Budapest Gambit

OTTO BORIK

Translated by Les Blackstock

B.T.Batsford Ltd, *London*

First published in German
as *Budapester Gambit* 1985
© Edition Mädler im Walter Rau Verlag,
Düsseldorf 1985
First English edition 1986
English translation © B.T.Batsford Ltd 1986

ISBN 0 7134 5297 8 (limp)

Photoset by Andek Printing, London
and printed in Great Britain by
Billing & Son Ltd, Worcester,
for the publishers
B.T.Batsford Ltd, 4 Fitzhardinge Street,
London W1H OAH

A BATSFORD CHESS BOOK
Adviser: R.D.Keene GM, OBE
Technical Editor: P.A.Lamford

Contents

Foreword

What should one play with Black?

Every chessplayer has asked himself this question. Should one follow the greats and base one's own repertoire on, say, the World Champion? Or should one adopt some aggressive variation to surprise the opponent?

The following considerations speak in favour of the second possibility:

Professionals have a lot of time to study countless variations and refine them deep into the middlegame. Furthermore, chess masters are 'transparent' inasmuch as their games are regularly published. The result of this is that they play only established variations which have been examined in detail; the consumption of time for this is considerable.

For the 'normal' league and tournament player the problem is quite different. He has not the advantage of ample time available for study, but also not the disadvantage that his own games are too well known and can be closely examined by his opponent. So he can play more enterprisingly and employ the element of surprise. And so we arrive at the theme of this book.

Every year hundreds of master games are published which open, for example, with the Benoni. If you play the Benoni it can easily happen that your opponent has just discovered a novelty in a magazine and uses it against you. Suddenly, instead of your (possibly weaker) opponent, you must struggle against Grandmaster X, which seldom turns out well.

The Budapest Gambit and Fajarowicz Gambit – the subjects of this book – are little played nowadays internationally; well informed professionals are hard to surprise there. At other levels, roughly up to 2200, one can be successful in many games with this surprise weapon, particularly if one is familiar with the most important ideas and combinations in this book. And if one meets a well-informed opponent (who knows this variation and perhaps has also read this book) then one must put up with a slight but defendable disadvantage; one also has to do that in many other openings with Black.

With this in mind: much success, and above all much fun with the combinational, fascinating Budapest/Fajarowicz Gambit!

Otto Borik

Symbols

+	Check
± ∓	Slight advantage
± ∓	Clear advantage
+− −+	Winning advantage
=	Level position
∞	Unclear position
!	Good move
!!	Outstanding move
!?	Interesting move
?!	Dubious move
?	Weak move
??	Blunder
corres	Correspondence
Ol	Olympiad
IZ	Interzonal
L	League
Ch	Championship
½f	Semi-final

Acknowledgments

The author would like to thank Les Blackstock who updated the German original and checked the proofs, and Bob Wade who provided valuable new material.

1 The Knight System 4 ♘f3

1	d4	♘f6
2	c4	e5
3	de	♘g4
4	♘f3 *(1)*	

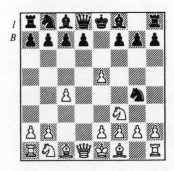

With this move White simul-
taneously protects the pawn on e5
and continues his development.
This quiet continuation is most
commonly played in the middle
and lower echelons of chess, but
also appears sometimes in international tournaments.

Black now has two important
continuations at his disposal:

A 4 ... ♘c6
B 4 ... ♗c5

In practice two other moves

occasionally appear:

a) **4 ... d6?** is an illogical gambit.
The main idea of the Budapest
Gambit consists above all in the
active posting of Black's KN on
e5, at the same time regaining the
sacrificed pawn. The move ... d6
only furthers Black's development
slightly, as the bishop is more
active on c5 or b4 than on d6.
After 5 ed ♗xd6 6 ♘c3 0-0 7 e3
♘c6 8 ♗e2 ♗f5 9 0-0 Black has no
compensation for the sacrificed
pawn, e.g. 9 ... ♕f6 10 h3 ♘ge5 11
♘d4 ♖ad8? (11 ... ♗g6? 12 f4 ♘d7
13 f5; 11 ... ♗d7 12 ♘db5 followed
by 13 ♘xd6 ±, and finally 11 ...
♘xd4 12 ed ♘g6 13 c5 ♗e7 14
♘d5) 12 ♘d5 ♕g6 13 ♗h5 1-0 in a
simultaneous game.

b) **4 ... ♗b4+**. This move has no
independent significance as it leads
by transposition of moves to a
position considered in the next
few pages. In all practical examples
... ♘c6 and ... ♘g(c)xe5 are played
later, reaching a basic position of
A1 (4 ... ♘c6).

A

4 ...   ♘c6

Black delays a decision on the development of his KB and immediately attacks the pawn on e5. Some theoretical works regard this move as dubious, but some recent analysis by Hungarian and Swedish masters has proved its viability.

White can defend his attacked pawn by 5 ♕d5 or 5 ♗f4. These both lead to variations considered later:

For 5 ♕d5 see Chapter 4: Rare 4th move continuations by White. After 1 d4 ♘f6 2 c4 e5 3 de ♘g4 4 ♕d5, we reach the present position with 4 ... ♘c6 5 ♘f3.

5 ♗f4 transposes to positions treated in Chapter 2.

We now examine:

A1 5 e3 ♗b4+ (and variations with a later ... ♗b4)
A2 5 e3 ♘gxe5
A3 5 ♗g5

A1

5   e3   ♗b4+

White now has three possibilities:

A11 6 ♗d2
A12 6 ♘c3
A13 6 ♘bd2

A11

6   ♗d2

An interesting game with this continuation was played a few years ago in an international tour-nament in Israel.

Game 1
Gutman-Shvidler
Beersheva 1982

(1 d4 ♘f6 2 c4 e5 3 de ♘g4 4 ♘f3 ♘c6 5 e3 ♗b4+ 6 ♗d2)

6	...	♗xd2+
7	♕xd2	0-0
8	♗e2	♘cxe5
9	♘xe5	♘xe5
10	0-0	d6
11	♘c3	♗g4
12	f3	♗e6
13	b3	♕h4
14	f4	

Better was 14 ♘d5 as after 14 ... ♗xd5 15 cd White exerts strong pressure down the c-file against the pawn on c7. 14 ... c6 followed by 15 ... ♖ad8 is safer, though White still has the more comfort-able game.

14	...	♘g4
15	♗xg4	♕xg4
16	♘b5	♖fc8
17	e4	♗d7
18	♘c3	♗c6
19	♖ae1	♖e8
20	♖e3	♕d7
21	♕d4	f5
22	♖fe1	fe
23	♘xe4	♖f8
24	♘g3	♖ae8
25	f5	*(2)*

25 ♕xa7? ♖a8 26 ♕d4 ♖xa2 and now 27 ♖e7 fails to 27 ... ♖xg2+ 28 ♔f1 ♕g4.

41	♘xe4	d5
42	cd	cd
	0-1	

2
B

25	...	♖xe3
26	♖xe3	b6
27	♖e6	♖e8
28	♘h5	♕f7
29	♕g4	

The situation seems critical for Black, but only if viewed superficially. He can easily defend g7 and with his next move removes the threat of ♘f6+.

29	...	♔f8
30	♘f4	♗d7
31	♖xe8+	♕xe8
32	♔f2?	

White parries the threat of ... ♕e1 mate but loses a pawn. He had to play 32 ♘e6+ ♗xe6 33 fe with a probable draw.

32	...	♕f7
33	h4	♕xf5
34	♕f3	c6
35	g4	♕c5+
36	♔g2	♔e7
37	♘d3	♕d4
38	♘f2	h5
39	♕e2+	♔d8
40	♕e4	♕xe4+

A12

6 ♘c3

Here Black can commit a serious error by not capturing the knight on c3 immediately. What can then happen is shown in the following game from the "golden age" of chess. The fact that the critical position is reached by transposition of moves is insignificant.

Game 2
Thomas-Reti
Baden-Baden 1925

(1 d4 ♘f6 2 c4 e5 3 de ♘g4 4 ♘f3 ♘c6)

5	♘c3	♘gxe5
6	e3	♗b4
7	♗d2	0-0
8	a3!	♗xc3
9	♗xc3	d6
10	♗e2	♘xf3+
11	♗xf3	♘e5
12	♗e2	♗e6
13	0-0	♕d7

The pawn on c4 is taboo: 13 ... ♗xc4? 14 ♗xc4 ♘xc4 15 ♕d4 ♘e5 16 f4! wins a piece.

14 c5!

The insecure position of the knight on e5 makes this advance possible, after which Black labours with a permanent weakness at d6.

| 14 | ... | ♖fd8 |

15	cd	♕xd6
16	♕xd6	cd
17	♖fd1	♖ac8
18	♖d4	♗c4
19	♔f1!	

White centralises his king for the coming endgame. Here one could conclude from the theoretical point of view with the assertion that White stands better and realised his advantage in 73 moves. However, we will continue, as a very interesting endgame with unusual points soon arises:

19	...	f6
20	♖ad1	♖c6
21	♗b4	♗b3
22	♖b1	

Better than 22 ♖xd6? ♖dxd6 23 ♖xd6 ♖c1+ followed by ... ♖b1.

22	...	d5
23	♔e1	♖dc8
24	♗c3	♘c4

The tactical threat ... ♘xa3 is easily parried by the pressure on the weakness at d5.

25	♗f3	♘b6

Not 25 ... ♘xa3 26 ba ♖xc3 27 ♖xb3! ♖xb3 28 ♗xd5+ and 29 ♗xb3.

26	♗d1	♗xd1

If Black avoids this exchange with 26 ... ♗c4, there follows 27 a4, 28 a5, 29 ♗f3 and 30 b3. The pawn on d5 is then systematically rounded up.

27	♖bxd1	♔f7
28	a4	♖c4

29	a5	♘a4
30	♖xc4	♖xc4

30 ... dc? 31 ♖d7+ followed by ♖xb7 naturally cannot be contemplated.

31	♖xd5	♘xc3
32	bc	♔e6
33	♖b5	♖c7
34	♔d2	♖d7+
35	♔c2	♔d6
36	f3	♔c6
37	c4	b6
38	g4	♖e7
39	ab	ab
40	♔d3 (3)	

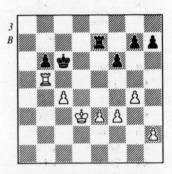

In this ending Black put up further heroic resistance but could no longer save the game.

40	...	♖a7
41	g5	fg
42	♖xg5	g6
43	h4	♖e7
44	h5	♖e6
45	f4	♔d7
46	♔d4	♖c6
47	f5	gf

48	♖g7+	♔e6
49	♖xh7	♖d6+
50	♔c3	♔e5
51	h6	♖e6
52	♖h8	♔e4
53	h7	♖e7
54	♔b4	♔xe3
55	♔b5	f4
56	♔c6!	

With the neat idea that if 56 ... f3 57 ♔d6 f2 (or rook any on the 7th rank, 58 ♖e8+ followed by h8♕; rook any on the e-file, 58 ♖f8 etc) 58 ♔xe7! f1♕ 59 ♖e8 and White will promote on h8.

56	...	♔f2
57	♔xb6	f3
58	♔c6	♖f7
59	c5	♔f1
60	♔b6	f2
61	c6	♔e2
62	♖e8+	♔d3
63	h8♕	f1♕
64	♖d8+	♔c2
65	♕h2+	♖f2
66	♕e5	♖f4
67	♕d5	♕e1

After 67 ... ♖b4+ 68 ♔c7 Black has no more checks. If 67 ... ♕f2+ 68 ♕c5+ with a winning rook ending.

68	♕d3+	♔c1
69	♕a3+	♔c2
70	♕c5+	♔b2
71	♖b8 *(4)*	

A pleasing point: 71 ... ♖b4+ 72 ♕xb4+! ♕xb4+ 73 ♔a7 and the c-pawn decides.

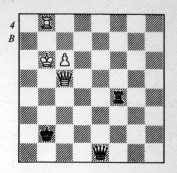

71	...	♖a4
72	♔c7+	♔a1
73	♖b3!	1-0

Black is either mated or cannot avoid an exchange of queens on c3, after which White wins easily with his c-pawn.

This example in no way casts doubt on ♗f8-b4. It only serves as a warning.

We notice that Black may not give up the bishop pair if he allows White to recapture on c3 with his bishop.

Thus we return to the position after 1 d4 ♘f6 2 c4 e5 3 de ♘g4 4 ♘f3 ♘c6 5 e3 ♗b4+ 6 ♘c3 and analyse the correct continuation for Black:

6	...	♗xc3+!
7	bc	♕e7!

By this means Black prevents c4-c5 and also ♗c1-a3.

8	a4	♘gxe5
9	♗a3	d6
10	c5	

White intends 10 ... dc 11 ♕d5,

regaining the pawn favourably, as 11 ... b6?? fails to 12 ♘xe5. However, Black has a surprise ready:

10	...	♘xf3+
11	gf	♕e5!
12	♕d2	dc
13	♗b5	♗d7
14	0-0	0-0-0

In the game Kamishov-Selyinsky, USSR 1973, White did not have sufficient compensation for the pawn and Black won an interesting game in 58 moves.

A13

6 ♘bd2

After the bishop check on Black's 5th move, White can also play 6 ♘bd2 as the East German grandmaster Rainer Knaak shows in the following game:

Game 3
Knaak-Adamski
Sandomierz 1976

(1 d4 ♘f6 2 c4 e5 3 de ♘g4 4 ♘f3 ♘c6 5 e3 ♗b4+ 6 ♘bd2)

6	...	♘gxe5
7	♘xe5	♘xe5
8	♗e2	

Here Black could have achieved a fully satisfactory game after 8 ... d5!? 9 cd ♕xd5 10 ♕a4+ ♘c6 11 ♗f3 ♕d6 12 0-0 0-0 13 ♖d1 ♕e7 and now it is very risky for White to take the pawn on offer: 14 ♗xc6 bc 15 ♕xc6 ♖b8 with a very dangerous attack after the build-up ... ♖b6, ... ♗b7, ... ♖g6 and ... ♗d6 – Trajković.

In the game Black continued too hurriedly:

8	...	♕h4?
9	0-0	0-0
10	♘b3	♖e8
11	♘d4	♘c6
12	♘f5	♕f6
13	♘g3	♗d6?!	(5)

Better was the re-grouping 13 ... ♗f8 followed by ... g6 and ... ♗g7. Such a set-up would firstly leave Black's kingside well secured, secondly would not leave the bishop on b4 cut off after an eventual d7-d6, and finally the pawn on g6 would take the squares h5 and f5 away from the knight on g3.

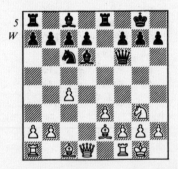

14	♘h5	♕e7
15	a3	a5
16	♗d2?!	

But now it is White who does not continue accurately. 16 f4! was better. The text move once again gives Black the opportunity to equalise: 16 ... ♗e5! 17 ♕c2 (or 17 ♖b1) 17 ... g6 18 ♘g3 a4! 19 ♗c3 d6. The Polish master, however, allows himself to be tempted by apparently easy booty.

16	...	♕e5?!
17	f4	♕xb2
18	♖b1	♕xa3
19	♖b3	♕a4
20	♗d3	♗f8
21	♗c3	

It is already too late for development by 21 ... d6: 22 ♘f6+! gf 23 ♗xh7+ ♔g7 (23 ... ♔xh7 24 ♕h5+ ♔g8 25 ♗xf6 etc; 24 ... ♔g7 25 ♖f3 followed by ♖g3) 24 ♗c2 followed by ♕h5 and/or ♖f3-g3 with an irresistible attack.

In view of the threat ♘f6+ Black must resort to 'indirect' moves.

21	...	♖e6
22	f5	♖e5
23	♖f4	d6
24	♖g4	♔h8
25	c5	♘b4
26	♗xe5	de
27	♘xg7!	

With the threat 27 ... ♗xg7 28 ♗b5! followed by ♕d8 and mate.

27	...	♕c6
28	♘h5	♗xc5
29	♗e4	♕d6
30	♕e1	♗d7
31	h3	♕h6
32	♖h4	♗c6
33	♗xc6	♘xc6

Or 33 ... ♕xc6 34 f6 threatening

♕b1 with an attack against the tender spot h7. Both players were in time-trouble here, which affects the logical flow of the game, but White's initiative cannot be shaken.

34	♖xb7	♗d6
35	♖b1	♗c5
36	♔h1	♕xe3

36 ... ♗xe3 loses the bishop after 37 ♘f4 ♕f6 38 ♘d5 or 37 ... ♕g5 38 ♖g4.

37	♘f6	♕xe1+
38	♖xe1	♔g7
39	♘h5+	♔h6
40	♘g3+	♔g7
41	♖c1	a4
42	♖xc5	a3
43	♖xc6!	

Better than 43 ♖c1 a2 44 ♖a1 ♘d4 followed by ... ♘b3.

43	...	a2
44	♖g4+	♔f8
45	♖c1	a1♕
46	♖xa1	♖xa1+
47	♔h2	1-0

Summary

The plan 4 ... ♘c6 and 5 ... ♗b4+ is not refuted in spite of the 2-1 score for White in the sample games just given.

After 6 ♘c3 Black must play ... ♗xc3+ immediately; after 6 ♘bd2 an early ... d5 promises equality. The most difficult position for Black arises after 6 ♗d2.

Black's task is significantly easier after the logical move 5 ...

♘gxe5, with which the next section is concerned.

A2
5 e3 (6)

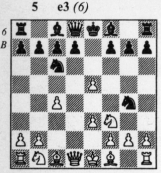

The bishop check on b4 and the variations connected with it were dealt with in A1. In this section we will examine a closely related continuation, namely the capture on e5. As already mentioned, the active posting of a black knight on e5 represents the basic idea of the Budapest Gambit.

For Black the question now arises: with which knight will he capture on e5?

A game of the Yugoslav Predrag Nikolić gives the answer in the form of the negative choice. It was played in the Junior World Ch in Mexico in 1979, where Nikolić, now a grandmaster, finished third behind Seirawan and Chernin. Already at that time Nikolić was a feared 'killer' in 1 d4 openings as he exploited every inaccuracy remorselessly.

Game 4
P.Nikolić-Barbero
Junior World Ch, Mexico 1979

(1 d4 ♘f6 2 c4 e5 3 de ♘g4 4 ♘f3 ♘c6 5 e3)

5 ... ♗c5

Patience please, capturing on e5 follows immediately.

6 ♘c3 ♘cxe5?

Only 6 ... ♘gxe5 is correct, as Nikolić shows at once.

7 h3!

Forces the exchange on f3, after which the White queen enters the game advantageously. The same applies when the moves ♘c3 and ... ♗c5 have been omitted.

A tip: either do not exchange on f3 at all, or only when White has played ♗e2 and therefore can no longer recapture with the queen.

7 ... ♘xf3+
8 ♕xf3 ♘e5
9 ♕g3

Here is an ideal post for the queen as it threatens the point g7 and therefore prevents the development of Black's kingside. As 8 ... ♕f6 is met by 9 ♘d5 with the unpleasant threats ♘xc7 or ♕xg7, Black must move his knight again. Thus seven of his first nine moves have been knight moves, which cannot be good!

9 ... ♘g6
10 ♗d2 ♗d6

After 10 ... 0-0 Black was afraid

of 11 h4.

11	f4	♗e7
12	0-0-0	♗f6
13	♕f3	d6
14	♘d5	0-0
15	♗d3	♗d7
16	h4	♖e8
17	h5	♘f8
18	g4	♗c6
19	g5	♗e7
20	♗c3	♗xd5
21	♕xd5	c6
22	♕d4	♘e6 (7)

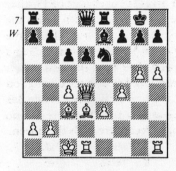

After the unfortunate opening Black was not at a disadvantage but then completely lost the thread. The following combination is a result of Black's series of inaccuracies.

23	♗xh7+!	♔xh7
24	♕e4+	♔g8
25	h6	

Nothing can repulse the threat 26 hg followed by ♕h7+ and mate: 25 ... g6 26 h7+ and h8♕ mate; the text also doesn't help.

25	...	♘xg5

26	hg!	1-0

Whoever plays over this game will never recapture on e5 with the c6 knight, will he?

After these experiences, **the correct order of moves** slowly crystallises:
(1 d4 ♘f6 2 c4 e5 3 de ♘g4 4 ♘f3 ♘c6)

5	e3	♘gxe5 (8)

Now 6 b3, 6 ♘c3 or 6 ♗e2 all lead by transposition to the main variation.

Only 6 ♕d5 has independent significance. The game Bergström-Hagen, corres 1962-63, continued 6 ... d6 7 ♘xe5 (White does not want to lose a tempo after ... ♗e6) 7 ... de! 8 ♕xd8+ ♘xd8 9 ♘c3 c6 10 ♗e2 ♗f5 11 0-0 ♘e6 12 b3 (12 e4 leaves an ugly hole on d4 where the black knight could settle) 12 ... ♗b4 13 ♗b2 0-0-0 and Black has a somewhat more pleasant endgame (14 a3 ♖d2!; 14 ♖fd1 ♗c2).

6	♗e2

6 ... ♗c5 transposes to the main variation of B.

6 ...   g6

Black obtains a satisfactory game with this plan of ... ♗g7, ... 0-0 and ... d6, as a game between two Dutch grandmasters makes clear.

Game 5
Sosonko-Ree
Amsterdam 1982

(1 d4 ♘f6 2 c4 e5 3 de ♘g4 4 ♘f3 ♘c6 5 e3 ♘gxe5 6 ♗e2 g6)

7	♘c3	♘xf3+
8	♗xf3	♗g7
9	♕d2	d6
10	b3	♘e5

A refined move. After the retreat 11 ♗e2 Black gets an active game with 11 ... ♕g5! 12 ♗f1 (12 g3 ♗h3; 12 0-0?? ♗h3) 12 ... ♗h3! *(9)*

The bishop is taboo because of ... ♘f3+; 13 ♖g1 also fails to ... ♘f3+ and 13 ... ♗xg2 is threatened.

We now examine:

a) **13 f4** ♕h4+ 14 ♔d1 (14 ♕f2? ♘d3+ 15 ♗xd3 ♗xc3+ etc; 14 g3 ♘f3+ 15 ♔d1 ♘xd2 16 gh ♗xc3) 14 ... ♗g4+ 15 ♔c2 ♘c6 and after ... 0-0-0 followed by ... ♖he8 Black is very active.

b) **13 ♘e4** ♕e7 14 ♗b2 (14 f4? ♘xc4!) 14 ... 0-0 15 0-0-0 ♗d7 followed by ... ♗c6 or even ... a5-a4 and Black has no complaints.

On account of this interesting tactical possibility, White played

11   ♗b2!

and after

11	...	♘xf3+
12	gf	0-0
13	0-0-0	♗h3

the chances were balanced.

14	♖hg1	♗e6
15	♘e4	f5
16	♘g5	♗xb2+
17	♕xb2	♕f6
18	f4	♕xb2+
19	♔xb2	♗f7
20	c5!	dc
21	♖d7	♖ad8!

The ending after 22 ♖xc7 ♖d2+ 23 ♔a3 b5! is good for Black.

22	♖gd1	♖xd7
23	♖xd7	h6
24	♘f3	♖c8
25	♘e5	♗e8
26	♖e7	♔f8
27	♖h7	♔g8
28	♖e7	♔f8
29	♖h7	♔g8 *(10)*

½-½

Neither side can improve their chances. A fighting draw, which unfortunately is not always the case these days between grandmasters.

Summary

Black does his best on his 5th move to recapture on e5 with his king's knight. After that he gets a satisfactory game with the set-up ... g6 and ... ♗g7.

A3

5 ♗g5 ♗e7 *(11)*

If White still had some problems

in A1 (after 5 ... ♗b4+), the way to equality in A2 (... ♘gxe5/... g6) is simple. A last possibility for White is the renunciation of the quiet 5 e3 in favour of the sharper continuation 5 ♗g5.

Apart from the exchange on e7, 6 ♗f4 is possible, which, after 6 ... ♗b4+, leads to a position which is examined in detail in Chapter 2.

Other moves scarcely come into consideration:

a) 6 h4 h6 7 ♗xe7 ♕xe7. The interpolation of the moves h7-h6 and h2-h4 is favourable for Black. Both sides have created an 'airhole', but Black can, in addition, use the square g4 for later operations.

b) 6 ♗d2 0-0 7 ♗c3 ♗c5 8 e3 ♕e7 9 ♕d5 ♖e8 followed by ... ♘gxe5 and ... d6 with a comfortable game for Black.

6 ♗xe7 ♕xe7
7 ♘c3

A venomous move. The Swedish masters Schüssler and Wedberg now give: 7 ... ♘cxe5? 8 ♘d5 ♕c5 9 e3 ♘xf3+ 10 gf ♘e5 11 f4 ♘g6 12 b4! ♕c6 13 ♕d4 with a winning position for White.

However, with the following precise move Black equalises immediately.

7 ... ♕c5!
8 e3 ♘gxe5 *(12)*

Schüssler and Wedberg now analyse:

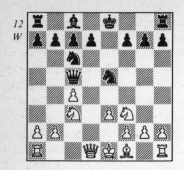

12
W

a) **9 ♘d5** 0-0 **10 ♕d2** (not 10 ♘xc7? ♕a5+ winning a piece) 10 ... ♘xf3+ **11 gf ♘e7 12 ♕d4** (If 12 b4 ♕d6 and White must still exchange on e7, but after that Black can advance actively with ... a5) 12 ... ♕xd4! **13 ♘xe7+ ♔h8 14 ed ♖e8** and Black regains the piece with a better ending on account of the weak white pawn structure.

b) **9 ♕d5 ♕e7 10 ♕d2 d6 11 ♘d5 ♕d8 12 0-0-0 0-0** followed by ... ♗e6 with equality.

Those who don't like this quiet position can fall back on a suggestion of the Hungarian Kaposztas who, instead of 8 ... ♘gxe5, makes a case for **8 ... 0-0** and gives the following variation: **9 ♕d5 ♘b4! 10 ♕b5 ♖e8 11 ♘d4 ♕e7**, again with equality, but with a full-blooded game for both sides. Worthy of examination are the complications after **12 ♘d5 ♕xe5 13 ♘f3 ♕d6 14 ♖d1** (threatening c4-c5) 14 ... a6 **15 ♕a4**

♘ce5. In any event 16 b4 is dangerous for White whose king cannot feel secure in the centre after 16 ... b5! 17 cb ♗b7. Further practical tests must be awaited here.

This ends the examination of the first section of the knight's variation. In B we will turn our attention to the sharper variation 4 ... ♗c5.

B

4	...	♗c5
5	e3	♘c6 *(13)*

13
W

We now examine:

B1 6 ♕d5
B2 6 a3
B3 6 ♗e2

Other possibilities:

a) **6 ♗d2** 0-0 7 ♗c3 ♕e7 8 a3 a5 or 8 ♕d5 ♖e8 with equality after the usual set-up ... ♘gxe5, ... d6 and ... ♗e6.

b) **6 b3 d6!** (exceptionally good here as 7 ed?? loses to 7 ... ♕f6) followed by ... ♘gxe5, transposing to variations with ♗e2 (B3).

B1

6 **♕d5**   **♕e7**
7 **a3**

This interpolation excludes the possibility of a check at b4 later. 7 ♘c3 ♘gxe5 8 ♗e2 d6 9 ♘e4 ♗e6 10 ♕d1 ♗b4+ 11 ♗d2 0-0-0 12 ♗xb4 ♘xb4 13 ♕b3 ♘xf3+ 14 ♗xf3 d5, Adler-Maroczy, Budapest 1896, was better for Black.

7 ...   **a5**
8 **♘c3** *(14)*

Or 8 ♗d2 0-0 9 ♗c3 ♖e8 10 ♗e2 ♘gxe5 11 0-0 d6 and after 12 ... ♗e6 Black stands well.

14
B

The critical position. Now:

a) **8 ... ♘gxe5** 9 ♘e4 d6 10 ♘xe5 ♘xe5 11 ♘xc5 dc. So far this is IM Minev analysing the game Popov-Tomov, Bulgaria 1959, in *ECO*. Minev believes Black has good counterplay, but unfortunately does not present any examples. There could follow 12 ♗e2 0-0 13 0-0 ♖d8 14 ♕e4 ♕f6. So far, certainly, a natural course of events. After 15 f4 ♘c6 (threatening

... ♗f5) 16 g4 'Black's good counterplay' is nowhere to be seen.

b) The following variation seems to give Black good chances: **8 ... 0-0!** (the pawn on e5 will not run away; first development is completed) 9 ♘e4 b6 10 ♘xc5 bc 11 ♗e2 (11 b3 ♖b8 12 ♖b1 ♗b7 threatening ... ♘d4) 11 ... ♗b7 12 0-0 ♖fb8 (again ... ♘d4 is threatened) 13 ♕d1 ♘cxe5. Black readily exchanges minor pieces and has pressure against the pawn on c4 and along the b-file.

We have seen that the sortie ♕d1-d5 often proves to be a loss of tempo with accurate play by Black.

B2

6 **a3**   **a5**
7 **b3**

This early development of White's QB is made possible by the interpolation of the moves a3 and ... a5; otherwise ... d6! would be played (see earlier note). Here 7 ... d6? would make no sense: 8 ed ♕f6 9 ♖a2.

7 ...   **0-0**
8 **♗b2**   **♖e8**
9 **♘c3**

It is clear from comparable examples already analysed that Black gets a good game after 9 ♕d5 ♕e7 followed by ... ♘gxe5, ... d6 and ... ♗e6.

9   ...   ♘gxe5
10 ♘xe5

10 ♗e2 just transposes after 10
... ♘xf3+ 11 ♗xf3 ♘e5 12 ♗e2.

10   ...   ♘xe5
11 ♗e2   d6 *(15)*

A natural and good move. The
sensational defeat of the Swedish
IM Akesson after 11 ... ♖a6?! will
be found in game 6.

Now 12 ♘a4 is not good
because of 12 ... ♕g5! – remember
game 5, Sosonko-Ree. Here it
could be worse: 13 0-0? ♗h3
winning the exchange; 13 g3 ♗h3
with advantage to Black; and
above all 13 ♗f1? ♗xe3!! 14 fe
♕xe3+ and wins:

a) 15 ♕e2 ♘d3+ 16 ♔d1 ♗g4 17
♕xg4 ♘f2+;

b) 15 ♗e2 ♘d3+ with mate or win
of the queen.

12   0-0

This is the main variation of this
section. IM Minev continues in
ECO with 12 ... ♗f5 and demonstrates a slight advantage for

White. The American Josef Staker,
the author of *The Budapest
Defence* (Chess Digest, 1982)
suggests the following improvement:

12   ...   ♖e6!? *(16)*

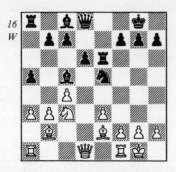

White has some superiority in
the centre and on the queenside
but lacks defenders of his king.
Thus the black rook heads for h6
to start a kingside attack in con-
junction with ... ♕h4.

We examine:

B21 13 ♘d5
B22 13 g3
B23 13 ♘a4

B21

13   ♘d5   ♖h6

The following example serves as
a demonstration of the danger of
Black's initiative: 14 b4? ♕h4
(Josef Straker gives 14 ... ab 15 ab
♖xa1 16 ♕xa1 ♕h4 17 h3 ♗xh3
and wins; an oversight in this
otherwise excellent work as White
mates with 18 ♕a8) 15 h3 ♗xh3 16

g3 ♖g6 17 ♘f4 ♗xe3! 18 ♔h1 (18 ♘xg6 ♕xg3+; 18 fe ♕xg3+ followed by ... ♗g2+ and mate) 18 ... ♗xf4! and Black mates in all variations, the prettiest being 19 gh ♗g2+ 20 ♔g1 ♘f3+ 21 ♗xf3 ♗xf3 mate. This crushing victory can naturally be traced back to the error 14 b4?; such a mistake could easily appear in tournaments not of the highest level.

| | 14 g3 | ♗h3 |
| 15 ♖e1 | c6!? |

On 15 ... ♕d7 there can follow:

a) **16 ♗f1?** ♗g4 17 ♗e2 ♗xe2 18 ♕xe2 ♕h3 with advantage to Black (19 f4 ♘d3!! 20 ♕xd3 ♕xh2+ followed by ... ♕xb2; 20 ♖f1 ♘xb2 21 ♕xb2 c6).

b) **16 ♘f4** g5! is also good for Black.

c) **16 ♗xe5** de 17 ♗f1 (as 17 ... ♗xf1?? naturally loses the queen to 18 ♘f6+) was played in Gould-Hardy, Leicester 1968, and now Staker gives 17 ... ♖e8 with equality. 17 ... c6 followed by ... ♖d6 and ... ♖d8 seems to give good chances.

d) **16 b4!** ♗a7 (16 ... ♗g2? is only a shot in the air – 17 ♘f4!) 17 ♘f4 ♖e8 18 ♗d4 is good for White however.

| 16 ♘f4 | ♗f5 |

16 ... ♕d7 17 b4! and if 17 ... ab 18 ab ♖xa1 19 ♕xa1 ♗xb4 20 ♘xh3 threatening ♕a8 and mate. Perhaps 16 ... ♕c8 is playable.

After 16 ... ♗f5 the chances are level. White must keep an eye on such Black possibilities as ... ♕c8, ... g5 and ... ♗e4.

B22

| 13 g3 | ♖h6 |
| 14 ♘e4 | |

14 ♘d5 transposes to B21.

| 14 ... | ♕d7 |

Otherwise Black loses a piece after ♘xc5 and ♗xe5. However, he now threatens ... ♕h3. As Black wins after 15 ♗xe5 ♕h3 16 g4 de 17 ♕d8+ ♗f8 or 15 ♘xc5 ♕h3, there remains ...

| 15 h4 | ♗a7 |

Bad is 15 ... ♗b6? 16 c5! or 15 ... ♕h3? 16 ♗xe5. Black now appears to hold the balance: 16 c5 ♕c6 17 ♗xe5 ♕xe4 or 17 cd ♕xe4 18 ♗xe5 ♕xe5 19 d7 ♗xd7 20 ♕xd7 ♗xe3!.

B23

| 13 ♘a4 | b6!? |

We will meet this motif in B3 – Black maintains the balance.

Attempts to win the apparently incarcerated bishop by b3-b4 meet with energetic resistance: 14 ♗c3 ♗d7 and now:

a) **15 b4?** ♗xa4! 16 ♕xa4 ab

b) **15 ♘b2** ♖h6 16 g3 ♗c6 17 b4 ♕c8! with the deadly threat ... ♕h3.

| 14 ♘xc5 | bc |
| 15 f4 | ♘d7 |

16	♗f3	♖b8
17	♕d3	

Still worse would be 17 e4 a4.

17	...	a4!

Black stands better. The fact that the moves a2-a3 and a7-a5 have been inserted here works clearly in favour of Black who exerts strong pressure on the b-file. After 18 ♗d1 ♕e7 19 ♖e1 ♗b7 Black has the advantage.

B3

6	♗e2	♘gxe5
7	0-0	0-0
8	♘xe5	

Or 8 b3 ♘xf3+ 9 ♗xf3 ♘e5 10 ♗e2 transposing.

8	...	♘xe5
9	b3	♖e8
10	♘c3 *(17)*	

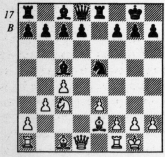

The main variation is 10 ... d6. The alternative 10 ... a5 will be discussed in the following game, about which a few words.

In August 1984 a very strong international open tournament took place in Berlin. Among the many title-holders taking part was the former European Junior Ch, Swedish IM Ralf Akesson. Akesson had finished second behind Hort in 1983 and was therefore regarded as one of the probable prizewinners. However, he lost his chance because of an absolutely unexpected loss to the little-known French lady player Nicole Tagnon – in the Budapest Gambit.

Game 6
Akesson-Tagnon
Berlin Open 1984

(1 d4 ♘f6 2 c4 e5 3 de ♘g4 4 ♘f3 ♗c5 5 e3 ♘c6)

6	♗e2	0-0
7	0-0	♖e8
8	♘c3	♘gxe5
9	b3	a5
10	♗b2	♘xf3+
11	♗xf3	♘e5

By one of the many move-orders we have reached the starting position of this section with the plan ... a5.

12	♗e2	♖a6 *(18)*

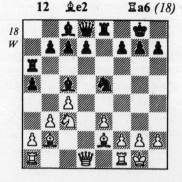

Black plans to swing the rook to the kingside to instigate an attack there. The threat of ... ♖h6 followed by ... ♛h4 requires energetic measures and at first the Swede shows himself to be fully on top of the situation.

13	♛d5!	♛e7
14	♘e4	♗a7
15	c5	♖g6
16	♖ac1	♗b8
17	f4	♘g4
18	♗xg4	♖xg4

With 19 ♘f2! White could simply exploit the exposed position of the rook (19 ... ♛xe3?? 20 ♗d4 ♛xf4 21 ♘xg4 ♛xg4 22 ♛xf7+) and build up his positional advantage (19 ... ♖g6 20 f5). The following pawn sacrifice should only lead to a draw.

19	♘g5?	♛xe3+
20	♔h1	♖xf4
21	♘xf7	c6
22	♘h6+	♔h8

... and draw by perpetual check one would think. But Akesson is not content with this . . .

23   ♛h5?

. . . and underestimates his opponent's clever reply . . .

23   ...   ♖ef8!

And now its over! 24 ♖fe1 fails to 24 ... ♛xe1+ and 25 ... ♖f1+ followed by mate or 24 ♖g1 to the game continuation.

24	♖xf4	♛xf4
25	♖g1	d5

26	cd	♗xd6

The knight on h6 remains trapped and White runs out of moves.

27   ♗c1

Or 27 ♗a1 (27 ♗c3) ... b6 followed by ... ♗c5 with a renewed threat on White's back rank (29 ♖e1 ♛f1+).

27   ...   ♛e5

0-1

Commentary based on notes by Claus-Dieter Meyer in *Schach 64* no 19/1984.

This game caused a great stir but White's loss says nothing about the correctness of the plan with ... a5. Rather it looks very much as if ... a5 is not completely satisfactory. [The variation was resuscitated in the game Oll-Romero, Groningen 1984-85, which went 10 ... a5 11 ♗b2 ♖a6 12 ♘e4 ♗a7 13 ♛d5 ♖ae6!! 14 ♛xa5 ♗b6 15 ♛c3 ♛h4 16 f4 ♖h6 17 h3 d5! 18 cd ♗xh3 and Black won in 30 moves – *tr.*] However it is important to be familiar with this idea, for in practical games it often happens that White makes some sort of harmless move and then this plan can certainly be employed. It is conceivable, and has actually happened in practice, for example, that White plays ♘bd2 instead of ♘c3; then ... a5 followed by ... ♖a6-h6 is very strong.

However, given that White plays the correct ♘c3, we return to the main variation.

10   ...   d6 *(19)*

19
W

In practice two plans have been tried:

B31 11 ♗b2, quietly continuing his development

B32 11 ♘a4, ridding himself of the bishop on c5.

B31

11   ♗b2   ♖e6

Strongly reminiscent of B2. It is in fact the same position without the moves a3 and ... a5. 12 ♘a4 leads to B32, and otherwise the game runs as in B2. The only difference lies in

12   g3

Now 12 ... ♖h6 would be bad because of 13 ♘e4 as the bishop on c5 cannot, by analogy with B2, retreat to a7.

What should Black play? Perhaps the retreat 12 ... ♖e8 followed by 13 ... ♗h3; perhaps 12 ... b6 followed by 13 ... ♗b7. One must return to these variations if the following suggestion proves a failure.

12   ...   ♕d7!? *(20)*

20
W

We already know the tricks after 13 ♘e4 ♖h6 from B2. We will look at another 'trap' – a pit into which White falls himself: 13 f4 ♗xe3+ 14 ♔h1 (with the intention 14 ... ♕c6+ 15 ♘d5 ♘d7 16 ♗f3 or 14 ... ♘c6 15 ♗g4) 14 ... ♖h6! and wins after ... ♖xh2+ and/or ... ♕h3+.

The move 12 ... ♕d7 seems at first rather odd, but on closer examination is quite logical as ... ♖h6 and ... ♕h3 is the ideal build-up to which to aspire. Due to lack of practical material, here is a 'constructed' conceivable variation.

13   ♗f3   ♘xf3+
14   ♕xf3   ♖h6
15   ♕g2   ♕g4

Black obtains an active game with ... ♕h5 and ... ♗h3 (on ♖fe1 then naturally ... ♗g4).

In all practical games White has decided to play ♘a4 to

liquidate the bishop pair and spoil Black's pawn structure.

B32

    11   ♘a4 *(21)*

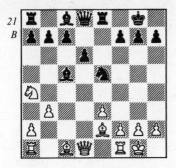

After 11 ... ♗b6 12 ♘xb6 ab 13 ♕d2 White's position is in fact somewhat more pleasant. He has many possibilities such as the plan ♗c3 and ♕b2 or ♖ae1, e4 and f4. [A recent example of this line saw Black achieve equality after 11 ... ♗b6 12 ♘xb6 ab 13 ♗b2 ♕h4 14 ♕d4 ♕xd4 15 ♗xd4 ♗g4 16 ♗xg4 (16 f3 ♘c6!) 16 ... ♘xg4, Karolyi-Rogers, Tallinn 1985 – *tr.*]

Black's stock rose again when the following game was published in which he introduced a highly original strategic idea.

Game 7
Osnos-Yermolinsky
Leningrad 1977

(1 d4 ♘f6 2 c4 e5 3 de ♘g4 4 ♘f3 ♗c5 5 e3 ♘c6 6 ♗e2 ♘gxe5 7 ♘xe5 ♘xe5 8 0-0 0-0 9 ♘c3 d6)

10	b3	♖e8
11	♗b2	a5
12	♘a4	b6!?
13	♘xc5	bc
14	f4	♘d7
15	♗f3	♖b8

The play on the half-open lines compensates Black for the bishop pair. The doubled pawns are no weakness at all here.

16	♕d2	a4
17	ba?	

Better was 17 ♕c3 f6 18 ♗c6 ab 19 ab ♗b7 with an unclear position. Black has the advantage after the column move.

17	...	♘b6
18	♖ae1	♗a6
19	♗e2	♖e4
20	♖f3	♘xc4
21	♗xc4	♗xc4
22	♖g3	f6
23	h3	♗f7
24	a5	c4
25	♕c2	d5
26	♕c3	c5
27	♕xf6	♕xf6
28	♗xf6	g6
29	♖d1	♖a8
30	♗c3	♖d8

There is nothing to be done about the breakthrough ... d4. White continues to fish in troubled waters.

31	a6	♖a8
32	h4	♖xa6
33	h5	♖a3
34	hg	hg

35	♗e5	d4
36	♖h3	♖xe5
37	fe	d3
38	e4	♖xa2
39	♖f3	♖e2
40	♖df1	d2
41	♖xf7	♖e1

0-1

The black king escapes the rook checks on h6. After 42 ♖d7 c3 followed by ... c2 the passed pawns prevail.

This ends the examination of the Knight System, the most popular variation of the Budapest Gambit.

2 The Bishop System 4 ♗f4

1	d4	♘f6
2	c4	e5
3	de	♘g4
4	♗f4 (22)	

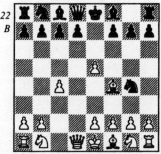

In the first chapter we saw White's queen's bishop generally developed on the a1-h8 diagonal after b3 and ♗b2. In this chapter we are concerned with a system in which White immediately develops this bishop on a different square.

Black does best in the Bishop System to follow the **main plan of the Budapest Gambit** which consists of four stages:

1. The king's bishop goes to c5 or b4. It makes room for castling and allows the later development ... ♕e7.

2. The queen's knight moves to c6. The pawn on e5 is eventually regained after ... 0-0, ... ♕e7 and ... ♖e8.

3. 3 ... ♕e7 is played and/or castles. The major pieces belong on the e-file.

4. With ... d6 and a move of the bishop on c8 development is ended.

About stage 1: In the knight's variation the bishop belonged on c5 or g7; ... ♗b4 was merely playable. In the bishop's variation the bishop always belongs on b4!

Please believe this above all; the evidence follows at once. Thus Black's further progress is clear: bishop to b4, knight to c6, queen to e7, castle and ... play.

The material divides as follows:

A 4 ... g5? Here an incorrect variation is 'shot down'.

B 4 ... ♘c6 5 ♘f3 ♗b4+ 6 ♘bd2. White takes care of his pawn structure and does not permit doubled pawns on the c-file.

C 4 ... ♘c6 5 ♘f3 ♗b4+ 6 ♘c3. Doubled pawns against the bishop pair – which prevails?

A

4   ...   g5? *(23)*

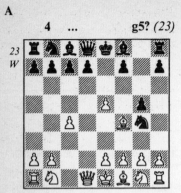

This move is repeatedly played, although it not only contradicts general strategic principles, but also the strategy of the Budapest Gambit, which, simply expressed, runs: *sound development with centralisation of a knight on e5.*

The move 4 ... g5 creates irreparable weaknesses in Black's camp and would only be justified by tactical circumstances which do not exist here as White has no weaknesses.

There are a number of good continuations for White. This book is not only intended for adherents of the Budapest Gambit, but also for 1 d4 players. For the first group an example will serve as a warning, for the second group a reliable method of combat.

5   ♗d2!

[Also promising is 5 ♗g3 ♗g7 6 ♘f3 ♘c6 7 ♘c3 ♘gxe5 8 ♘xe5 ♘xe5 9 e3 d6 10 h4! h6 11 c5, Schüssler-Herrera, Havana 1985 –

tr.]

5   ...   ♘xe5

5 ... ♗g7 6 ♘c3 ♘xe5 transposes to the main variation. 6 ... ♗xe5 7 ♘f3 ♗xc3+ 8 ♘xc3 is obviously good for White.

6   ♗c3   ♗g7
7   e3 *(24)*

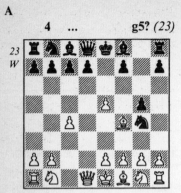

The main threat is f4 winning a piece. In all known games Black now played 7 ... g4, the only exception being Lorenz-Greger, West Germany 1975: 7 ... 0-0 8 h4 g4 9 ♘e2 d6 10 ♘g3 ♘bc6 11 ♕c2 f5 (directed against ♘f5) 12 ♘h5 ♗h8 13 ♘d2 ♗e6 14 f4 ♘g6 (14 ... gf 15 gf followed by ♗e2, 0-0-0 and ♖dg1 looks very risky for Black) 15 ♗xh8 ♘xh8 (15 ... ♔xh8?? 16 ♕c3+ etc) 16 ♕c3 ♕e7 17 0-0-0 ♘g6 18 ♗d3 ♖ae8 (18 ... ♘xh4?? 19 ♖xh4) 19 e4 ♖f7 20 ♖de1 ♘xh4 (20 ... ♕f8 21 ef ♗xf5 22 ♖xe8+ ♕xe8 23 ♗xf5 ♖xf5 24 ♘f6+) 21 g3 fe (21 ... ♘g6 22 ef as before) 22 ♘xe4 ♘f3 23 ♘ef6+ ♔f8 24 ♘d5 1-0.

7   ...   g4

8	♘e2	d6
9	♘f4	h5

Preventing ♘h5, which can be very disruptive as we have just seen.

10 ♕c2 *(25)*

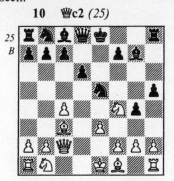

10 ...   ♕g5

In his book *The Budapest Defence* Josef Staker suggests this improvement.

Henneberke-Bakonyi, Holland v. Hungary 1949, continued 10 ... ♘a6 11 ♘d2 ♘c5 12 ♘e4 b6 13 ♘xc5 bc 14 ♗d3! with advantage to White. Black cannot castle because of the weakness on h5. White plays ♗e4, 0-0-0 and h3.

11 ♘d2   ♗f5 *(26)*

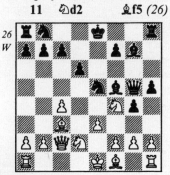

The author now continues with 12 e4(?) ♗e6 and assesses the position quite correctly as open. However, White can play better.

12	♕b3	b6
13	c5!	0-0

This is the only reasonable move. 13 ... bc?? 14 ♕b7 loses for Black, as does 13 ... dc? 14 ♗xe5 ♗xe5 15 ♕d5.

14	cd	cd
15	h4	

The win of a pawn after 15 ♕d5 ♘bc6 16 ♕xd6 ♖ad8 would be very questionable.

15 ...   ♕h6

15 ... gh 16 ♘xh3 cannot be good.

16	g3	♘bc6
17	♗g2	♖ac8
18	0-0	

White stands clearly better. His king position is rock solid and all his pieces stand well. There are two permanent weaknesses in Black's camp to exploit (h5 and d6); the latter will soon become a target for the white rooks on the d-file. The knight on d2 will move to e4. The rest of the game will be very pleasant.

B

4	...	♘c6
5	♘f3	♗b4+
6	♘bd2	♕e7 *(27)*

Here White has two main alternatives:

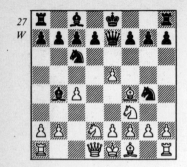

27
W

B1 7 e3
B2 7 a3

B1

7   e3

Schüssler and Wedberg give a convincing equalising line against this.

7   ...   ♘gxe5
8   ♘xe5

Or 8 a3 ♘xf3+ 9 gf ♗xd2+ 10 ♕xd2 d6 11 ♖g1, van Scheltinga-Adema, Holland 1938. Black can obtain a fully satisfactory game with 11 ... ♘e5 12 ♗e2 f6 followed by ♗d7-c6.

8   ...   ♘xe5
9   ♗e2

9 a3 transposes to B2.

9   ...   0-0
10   0-0   d6

[Less accurate is 10 ... ♗xd2 11 ♕xd2 d6 12 ♖fd1 b6 13 b4 ♗b7 14 c5 dc 15 bc ♘g6 16 ♕d7 ♕xd7 17 ♖xd7 ± Garcia Palermo-Rogers, Reggio Emilia 1984-85 – *tr.*]

11   ♘b3

Or 11 ♘f3 a5 followed by ... ♗c5 with equality.

11   ...   b6
12   a3   ♗c5

With an equal game after 13 ♘d4 a5 or 13 ♘xc5 bc followed by ... a5, ... f6, ... ♗e6 and play on the b-file. We recall that we have seen this motif several times, e.g. in Game 7.

If White plays 14 b4 immediately, Black must reply 14 ... ♘d7! followed by ... a5 with a good game.

B2

7   a3 *(28)*

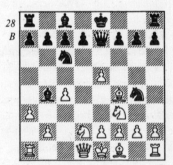

28
B

7   ...   ♘gxe5!

The famous "Kieninger trap". The late German master Georg Kieninger once used it in an offhand game against Godai at Vienna 1925. There followed 8 ab?? ♘d3 mate. This example was henceforth quoted in many chess books, though also under other names, for later many more players were to fall into the "Kieninger trap".

8   ♘xe5   ♘xe5

Another invitation to self-mate after 9 ab?? ♘d3.

9   e3

Or 9 ♗xe5 ♗xd2+ (Black must now exchange as he no longer has a knight to give mate on d3!) 10 ♕xd2 ♕xe5 with equality:

a) **11 e3** b6 12 ♗e2 ♗b7 13 0-0 0-0-0

b) **11 g3** 0-0 12 ♗g2 ♖e8 13 e3 d6 14 0-0 ♗e6 (15 ♗xb7? ♖ab8 and 16 ... ♖xb2; 15 ♖ac1 =).

9   ...   ♗xd2+
10 ♕xd2   d6
11 ♗e2   0-0

[Black could also consider castling queenside, e.g. 11 ... b6 12 e4 ♗b7 13 f3 0-0-0 14 0-0-0 f6 15 h4 h5 16 ♖he1?! ♖hg8 17 ♕c3 g5 18 hg fg 19 ♘h2 g4 20 f4 ♘d7 21 ♗d3 h4, Browne-Speelman, Taxco IZ 1985 (0-1, 41). Browne suggests 16 ♔b1 ♖dg8 17 b4 g5 18 hg fg 19 ♗e3 gives White a small edge – *tr.*]

12   0-0   b6!?

Also playable is 12 ... a5 which has often been tried by the Hungarian Kaposztas. The text move seems more accurate; Black does nothing loosening and first completes his development. [A recent example is 12 ... a5 13 ♖c1 b6 14 b3 ♗b7 15 ♗g3 ♖fe8 16 ♖c3 ♘d7 17 f3!? ♕g5 18 ♗d3 ♕c5 19 ♖b1 ♔h8, Korchnoi-Kaposztas, Berlin 1985. White won a long

positional struggle in 66 moves. – *tr.*]

13   b4   ♗b7 *(29)*

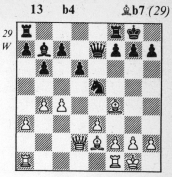

Game 8
Lukacs-Schüssler
Tuzla 1981

14   ♗g3

a) Another example from a recent tournament, Carlesson-Wedberg, Sweden 1977, continued **14 ♖ac1** ♘d7 15 ♕d1 a5 16 ♗f3 ♗e4 17 ♗xe4 ♕xe4 18 ♕d5 ♖fe8 19 ♖fd1 h6 20 ♖d4 ♕e7 21 ♕c6 ab 22 ab ♘f8! 23 ♖dd1 ♘e6 24 ♗g3 ♕f6 *(30)*

Unfortunately IM Tom Wedberg does not quote any more of his game. He only maintains that

Black stands better. White cannot become active with c4-c5 and Black is left in peace to harry the white queenside weaknesses after ... ♖d8, ... ♖a2, ... ♖da8, ... ♖8a3 and ... ♖b2.

b) There is also a noteworthy analysis by Schüssler and Wedberg: **14 c5?!** dc 15 bc. Acceptance of the pawn sacrifice would suit White: 15 ... ♕xc5? 16 ♖fc1 ♕e7 (or ... ♕d6) 17 ♕c3 regaining the pawn advantageously (17 ... ♘c6 18 ♗f3!). However, Black consistently follows his dark-squared strategy: 15 ... ♖fd8! 16 ♕c3 ♖d5! 17 cb ab 18 ♖fc1 ♖c5 19 ♕b2 ♖aa5. Black stands well and can win quickly if White plays carelessly, e.g. 20 ♖c3 ♘g6 21 ♗g3 h5 22 h3 h4 23 ♗h2 ♖g5 24 ♗f1 ♕e4 25 f3 ♕xf3 26 ♗xc7 ♕xh3 27 ♗xb6 ♖ab5! 28 ♖b3 (28 ♕xb5 ♖xg2+!) 28 ... ♖xg2+! 29 ♗xg2 ♖g5 30 ♖a2 ♕e6! etc.

After the text move, the white bishop anticipates being jostled by ... ♘g6, but above all White wants to advance his e- and f-pawns. A possible line is 14 ... h6 15 ♖fe1 ♖fe8 16 e4! (16 ... ♗xe4? 17 ♗f1! f5 18 f3 ♗b7 19 f4) 16 ... ♘d7 17 ♗d3 followed by f4. Even this position is not particularly bad for Black, but the text move avoids all such problems.

| 14 | ... | ♘d7 |
| 15 | ♖fe1 | a5 |

| 16 | ♗f1 | f5 |

Black could also play 16 ... ♖a7 immediately, followed by 17 ... ♖fa8.

17	f3	♖a7
18	♕d4	♖fa8
19	♖ab1	

Not 19 b5? ♘c5 followed by ... ♖f8, ... ♖a8-e8. The knight has a dream square on c5.

| 19 | ... | ab |
| 20 | ab | ♖a3 (31) |

For reasons of tournament tactics, the players did not tempt fate in this equal position.

½-½

So after the quiet continuation 6 ♘bd2 Black has no problems. Therefore the sharper 6 ♘c3 is often tried and has provided much practical material. This continuation is examined in C.

C

4	...	♘c6
5	♘f3	♗b4+
6	♘c3	♗xc3+

7 bc ♛e7 (32)

If Black regains the pawn on e5 he can play for a favourable ending on account of White's pawn weaknesses. Therefore the continuation is practically forced.

8 ♛d5 f6

There is no time for 8 ... 0-0 because of 9 h3.

9 ef ♞xf6

Three retreats come into consideration:

C1 10 ♛d3
C2 10 ♛d2
C3 10 ♛d1

C1

10 ♛d3 (33)

10 ... d6
11 e3

11 g3 ♞e4 12 ♗g2 ♞c5 13 ♛c2 ♞a5 14 ♞d2 ♗e6 15 ♗d5 0-0 16 ♗e3 c6 17 ♗xe6+ ♛xe6 18 ♗xc5 dc 19 e3 ♛h3 with better chances for Black – Schüssler and Wedberg.

11 ... ♞e4
12 ♗e2 0-0 (34)

Our illustrative game No. 9 continues with 13 ♞d4. One can wonder why White does not play the obvious 13 0-0. The answer lies in the excellent analysis of the Swedish masters in the magazine *Schacknytt:*

13 0-0 ♗g4!

It fits in with Black's plan to exchange minor pieces (in particular the bishop on e2) for he can then set to work on the doubled pawns on the c-file.

14 ♞d4

On any neutral move, such as 14 ♖fd1, Black realises the ideal set-up with ... ♞c5, ... ♞a5 and ... ♛f7.

14 ... ♞c5

Setting the trap 15 ♘xc6? bc 16 ♕d1 ♗xe2 17 ♕xe2 ♖xf4!.

15	♕d1	♗xe2
16	♕xe2	♘a5
17	♖ab1	b6

After 18 ... ♕f7 followed by ... ♘xc4 Black stands better.

The final position demonstrates impressively how a doubled pawn should be 'gripped'.

Some months after the publication of this analysis the Yugoslav GM Milan Vukić and the Australian IM Ian Rogers met in the New Year tournament at Reggio Emilia. Both were acquainted with the above analysis, so it is not surprising that White avoided the unpleasant exchange of light-squared bishops.

Game 9
Vukić-Rogers
Reggio Emilia 1983-84

(1 d4 ♘f6 2 c4 e5 3 de ♘g4 4 ♗f4 ♘c6 5 ♘f3 ♗b4+ 6 ♘c3 ♗xc3+ 7 bc ♕e7 8 ♕d5 f6 9 ef ♘xf6 10 ♕d3 d6 11 e3 0-0 12 ♗e2 ♘e4)

But not immediately 12 ... ♗g4 because after 13 h3 ♗xf3 14 ♗xf3 the square e4 is not available for the black knight and he therefore cannot carry out the promising manoeuvre ... ♘e4-c5.

13	♘d4

This way ... ♗g4 is radically prevented.

13	...	♘c5

14	♕d1	♘e5 (35)

35
W

14 ... ♘a5 would be inaccurate here because of 15 ♘b3! and White could exchange one of the enemy knights.

After the text move 15 ♘b3 would no longer be so good: 15 ... ♘e6 16 ♗g3 b6 followed by ... ♗b7. The knight would have no future on b3 and would have to return. Moreover, the formation of the black pawns on b6 and d6 is 'poison' for the doubled pawns which White can never dissolve.

15	0-0	♔h8
16	♖c1	♗d7
17	♕c2	♕f7

How does White protect the pawn on c4? Apart from the text move 18 ♘b3 still comes into consideration with the idea 18 ... ♘xc4? 19 ♘xc5 dc 20 ♗xc4 ♕xc4 21 ♗xc7, but Black can play better: 18 ... ♗f5 19 ♕d1 (19 ♕b2 ♘cd3) 19 ... ♘cd7 followed by ... ♗e6.

18	♗xe5	de
19	♘f3	♕e7

20	♘d2	♗c6
21	♗f3	e4
22	♗e2	♖f6
23	♘b3	♖h6
24	♘xc5	♕xc5
25	♖cd1	♕e5
26	h3	

26 g3? ♕e6 and ... ♕h3.

| 26 | ... | ♕g5 |
| 27 | ♗g4 | ♖g6 |

Threatening ... h5, so White prevents this with his next move.

| 28 | ♕e2 | ♕a5 |

½-½

The players agreed a draw on account of the variation 29 ♗d7 ♕g5 (29 ... ♗xd7? 30 ♖xd7 ♕g5 31 ♕g4 ♕xg4 32 hg ♖c6 33 ♖fd1 ♖g8 34 ♖1d4!) 30 ♗g4 ♕a5 31 ♗d7 ♕g5 with repetition of moves.

C2

| 10 | ♕d2 | d6 |
| 11 | e3 (36) | |

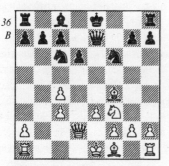

36
B

Stahlberg lost with the slow build-up 11 ♘d4 0-0 12 f3 ♗d7

13 e4 to Richter at Swinemünde 1930: 13 ... ♘xe4 14 fe ♘xd4 15 ♗e3 (15 ♕xd4 ♖xf4; 15 cd ♕xe4+ 16 ♗e3 ♖ae8) 15 ... ♘e6 followed by ... ♗c6 and ... ♖ae8. White's position is hopeless.

| 11 | ... | 0-0 |
| 12 | ♘d4 | |

12 ♗e2 ♗g4 will transpose to C1.

After 12 ♗d3 ♘e5 13 0-0 ♘xf3+ 14 gf ♗h3, van den Broeck-Trajković, Vienna 1953, Black had a good game, e.g. 15 ♖fd1 ♘d7 16 ♗e4? g5 17 ♕d5+ ♔h8 18 ♗g3 (18 ♗xg5? ♖g8 and ... h6) 18 ... ♘c5 with numerous possibilities for Black, such as ... h5, ... ♗e6, ... ♖ae8 etc. White would have to play 16 ♗f1 but after 16 ... ♗xf1 17 ♖xf1 ♘c5 Black still has an excellent game.

12	...	♘e5
13	♗e2	♘e4
14	♕c2	

14 ♕d1 ♘c5 transposes to game 9.

| 14 | ... | ♘c5 |
| 15 | 0-0 | b6 |

with a good game for Black, e.g. 16 ♘b3 ♘cd7 followed by ... ♕f7, ... a5 and ... ♗a6.

C3

| 10 | ♕d1 | |

White retreats to a square where he cannot be attacked by a knight, as on d3 or d2.

Game 10
Inkiov-Djukić
Bor 1983

(1 d4 ♘f6 2 c4 e5 3 de ♘g4 4 ♘f3
♘c6 5 ♗f4 ♗b4+ 6 ♘c3 ♗xc3+ 7
bc ♕e7 8 ♕d5 f6 9 ef ♘xf6)

10	♕d1	d6
11	e3	0-0
12	♗e2	♘e4
13	♖c1	♔h8

[13 ... ♗g4 14 0-0 ♔h8,
Campos-Akesson, Valjevo 1984,
may be more accurate – *tr.*]

14	0-0

[Rogers gives 14 ♘d2! ♘c5 15
♘b3 ♘e4 16 0-0 as an improvement
– *tr.*]

14	...	g5
15	♗g3	h5 (37)

Hardly orthodox! Black threatens
to trap the bishop by ... h4, and
the usual procedure in this sort of
position, namely h3 or h4, fails to
16 ... ♘xg3 17 fg ♕xe3+.

16	♗d3	♘c5

16 ... h4 is refuted by 17 ♗e5+!

♘xe5 18 ♗xe4.

17	h4

[Rogers gives 17 ♘h4 gh 18
♕xh5+ ♔g8 19 ♗xh4 ♕g7 as
unclear – *tr.*]

17	...	♖xf3!! (38)

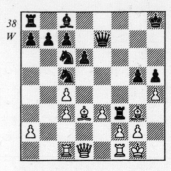

18	gf

Perhaps White should reluctantly
accept the following variation: 18
♕xf3 ♗g4! (much better than 18
... ♘xd3 19 ♕xh5+) 19 ♕d5 ♗e6
20 ♕f3 ♘xd3 21 ♕xh5+ ♕h7 22
♕xh7+ ♔xh7 23 ♖cd1 gh 24
♗xh4 ♗xc4. Naturally White
stands worse here but in the game
he succumbs in a few moves to a
furious attack by the Yugoslav
master.

18	...	gh
19	♗h2	

[Rogers queries this and gives as
White's only chance 19 ♗f4 ♗h3
20 ♔h2 ♗xf1 21 ♗xf1 ♘e6 22
♕d5! – *tr.*]

19	...	♗h3
20	♔h1	♖g8!
21	♖g1	♖xg1+

[These moves were all repeated in Lanzani-Rogers, Nuoro 1984, and at this point White resigned! – *tr.*]

22	♕xg1

22 ♔xg1 ♕g7+ 23 ♗g3 hg is even worse for White.

22	...	♘xd3
23	♖d1	♕f7
24	♗f4	

Or 24 f4 ♕xc4 threatening ... ♕e4+.

24	...	♘xf4
25	gf	♕xf4

As Black wins quite sadistically after 26 ♖d3 ♘e5 27 ♖e3 b6 28 ♕e1 ♗e6, White prefers the end with horror to the horror without end.

26	♕g6	♕xf3+
27	♔h2	♕xd1
28	♕f6+	♔g8

0-1

The Bulgarian GM could now convince himself that the black king wanders to d7. Then diagonal checks are prevented by the bishop on h3 and check on the seventh rank can be parried by ... ♘e7.

Summary

After the moves **1 d4 ♘f6 2 c4 e5 3 de ♘g4 4 ♗f4** the Bishop System arises. Black is well advised first of all to leave the bishop on f4 in peace. As we have seen in A, 4 ... g5? irrevocably weakens one's own position. Pieces can return after an unsuccessful excursion, but pawns cannot.

The best method is **4 ... ♘c6 5 ♘f3 ♗b4+**. After 6 ♘bd2 the d-file is blocked, so the white queen cannot hurry to the help of the pawn on e5. Black then plays 6 ... ♕e7 and regains the sacrificed pawn with a satisfactory game.

After 6 ♘c3 White can indeed hold the pawn on e5 but only at the cost of shattered pawns on the c-file. Subsequently Black plays ... f6, accepting to play on a pawn down, but he gets compensation for this in pressure on the e- and f-files.

3 The Alekhine System 4 e4

1	d4	♘f6
2	c4	e5
3	de	♘g4
4	e4	*(39)*

In the first chapter White protected the accepted gambit pawn by 4 ♘f3 and in the second chapter by another method 4 ♗f4. In both cases Black regained the gambit pawn.

In the Alekhine system White returns the booty immediately and strives for superiority in the centre.

The White pawn structure e4/c4 assures White a strong point on d5, but his light-squared bishop is somewhat limited in mobility. In some variations dark-square weaknesses can arise in White's camp. It is generally considered a rule in this system that exchange of dark-squared bishops is favourable for Black.

Black can protect the attacked knight (4 ... h5), continue in gambit style (4 ... d6) or recapture on e5 (4 ... ♘xe5). The main possibilities are:

A 4 ... **h5**
B 4 ... **d6 5 ed**
C 4 ... **d6 5 ♗e2**
D 4 ... **♘xe5 5 f4 ♘g6**
E 4 ... **♘xe5 5 f4 ♘ec6**

Other continuations:

a) **4 ... ♕h4??** 5 g3 ♕h5 6 ♗e2 d6 7 h3 winning a piece.

b) **4 ... ♘xf2??** 5 ♔xf2 ♕h4+ 6 g3 ♕xe4 7 ♘f3 ♗c5+ 8 ♔g2 and after ♘c3 followed by ♘d5 White is winning.

c) Untested here is **4 ... ♗b4+** after which White must find the best of three possible continuations:

c1) **5 ♘c3 ♘xe5 6 f4 ♘g6** transposes to D.

c2) **5 &d2 &xd2+ 6 ♕xd2 ♘xe5 7
♕c3 ♕e7** (7 ... ♘bc6 8 f4 wins the
pawn on g7) with a good game for
Black. 8 f4 now gets White into
difficulties (8 ... ♘g6 9 ♕xg7?
♕xe4+) and after the plausible
continuation 8 ♘d2 0-0 9 &e2
♘bc6 10 ♘gf3 d6 11 0-0 f5 Black is
active. Remember the above rule
referring to the exchange of dark-
squared bishops.

c3) **5 ♘d2 ♘xe5 6 a3** seems to be
favourable for White. 6 ... &xd2+
7 &xd2 followed by 8 &c3 is
obviously advantageous for White
and after 6 ... &e7 (6 ... &c5 7 ♘b3)
7 ♘b3 or 6 ... &e7 7 f4 ♘ec6 (7 ...
♘g6) 8 ♘df3 followed by &d3
and ♘e2 White is better developed.

A

    4   ...   **h5?!** *(40)*

This move contains some traps.
For example 5 ♘f3 &c5 or 5 f4?
&c5 6 ♘h3 ♘c6 (7 &e2? ♕h4+)
are good for Black.

We see here the only advantage

of the move ... h5, namely the
continued pressure against f2. It
is therefore natural to drive the
knight on g4 away. Later in the
game ... h5 will prove a weakness
on Black's kingside. For example,
short castling is temporarily prevented. Now:

A1 5 h3

A2 5 &e2

A1

    5   **h3**

Game 11
Ahues-Helling
Berlin 1932-33

(1 d4 ♘f6 2 c4 e5 3 de ♘g4 4 e4 h6)

5	**h3**	**♘xe5**
6	**&e3**	**&b4+**
7	**♘d2**	**f5**

Later this move was quite rightly
criticised, though Black also stands
worse after other moves. *ECO*
mentions 7 ... b6 but after 8 ♕b3
&e7 9 0-0-0 &b7 10 f4 ♘g6 11
♘gf3 ♘c6 12 c5! White stands
better, e.g. 12 ... 0-0 13 ♕d5!
followed by ♕xh5 or 12 ... ♖b8 13
♕c3 0-0 14 g4!.

8	a3	&e7
9	♕b3	♘a6
10	0-0-0	d6
11	c5!	♘xc5
12	&xc5	dc
13	♘c4	&g5+
14	♔b1	♕e7
15	♘xe5	♕xe5

16 ♘f3 (41)

Black is lost. **16 ...** ♛xe4+ fails to 17 ♗d3 e.g. 17 ... ♛f4 18 g3 ♛xf3?? 19 ♗b5+ followed by 20 ♛xf3.

16 ... ♛e7 17 ef ♗xf5+ 18 ♗d3 ♗xd3+ 19 ♛xd3 threatening ♛g6+ and ♖he1+ is completely hopeless for Black.

There only remains **16 ...** ♛f6 17 ♗d3 (here 17 ef ♗xf5+ 18 ♗d3 would not be so good because of 18 ... 0-0-0; the queen being on f6 rather than e7 protects the bishop on f5) 17 ... f4 18 e5 ♛h6 (otherwise ♗g6+) 19 ♗e4 ♗e6 (19 ... c6 20 ♖d6; 19 ... ♖b8 20 ♛a4+ followed by ♛xa7) 20 ♛b5+! c6 21 ♛xb7 0-0 22 ♖d6 ♖ae8 23 ♛xc6 threatening ♘xg5 followed by ♖xe6 and if 23 ... ♗d8 24 ♖xe6 followed by ♗d5.

A2

5 ♗e2

After 4 ... h5, 5 h3 is good enough but one must also examine 5 ♗e2

on account of the following move order: 4 e4 d6 5 ♗e2 and only now 5 ... h5.

After 5 ♗e2 Black has two possibilities:
A21 5 ... ♗c5
A22 5 ... d6

A21

5 ... ♗c5

Game 12
Golombek-Tartakower
Birmingham 1951

(1 d4 ♘f6 2 c4 e5 3 de ♘g4 4 e4 h5 5 ♗e2 ♗c5)

6 ♘h3

6 ♗xg4 ♛h4! 7 g3 ♛xg4 8 ♛xg4 hg gives Black superb play for the pawn on account of the open h-file and the light-square weaknesses in White's position. 8 f3 ♛e6 9 f4 d6 and later ... h4 also gives Black excellent chances.

6 ... ♘xe5
7 ♗g5 ♗e7

On 7 ... f6 White naturally plays not 8 ♗xh5+ because of 8 ... g6, but 8 ♗d2 h4 9 ♗c3 and subsequently ♘f4, as in the game.

8 ♗xe7 ♛xe7

It is true that the exchange of the dark-squared bishops is pleasant for Black but here this plus has been bought at some price in view of the permanent weakness at h5 and the loss of tempo ♗c5-e7.

9 0-0 d6

10	♘f4	c6
11	♘c3	

After the risky continuation 11 ♘xh5?! g6 12 ♘g3 ♛h4 13 h3 Black has a strong attack on the h-file. If he wants he can even force a draw by 13 ... ♗xh3 14 gh ♛xh3 15 ♖e1 ♛h2+ 16 ♔f1 ♛h3+ etc.

11	...	♗g4
12	f3	♗d7

Black has been able to save his pawn on h5 and control the square d5 but these measures have cost him time. White has a great space advantage.

13	♛b3	b6
14	♛a3	

Setting his sights on the weakness on d6.

14	...	♖h6
15	b3	♛f6
16	♛c1	♘a6
17	♖d1	0-0-0 *(42)*

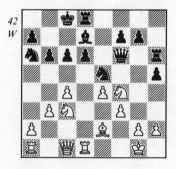

42
W

| 18 | ♘b5! | |

This knight is immune: 18 ... cb 19 cb+ ♔c5 (19 ... ♘c7?? 20 ♘d5) 20 ♘d5 ♛e6 21 b4. White regains

the piece, has a magnificent out-post on d5 and the possibility of opening up the black king quickly by a4-a5.

18	...	♗e8
19	♘d4	g5
20	♘h3?	

A mistake in a superior position. 20 ♘d3! would have maintained the advantage, e.g. 20 ... g4 21 ♘f5 ♖g6 22 f4 with a clear advantage to White.

20	...	g4!
21	♘f5	♖g6
22	♘f4	gf!
23	♛a3	fe
24	♛xa6+	♔b8
25	♘xe2	♛g5
26	g3	♛g4
27	c5	b5
28	♘c3	h4
29	♖xd6	♖dxd6
30	cd	hg
31	♘xg3	♘f3+
32	♔f2	♘xh2
33	♘ce2	♛f3+
34	♔e1	♖xg3
35	♛a5	♔b7

The black king flees from the threat of ♛c7+ followed by ♛c8 mate.

36	♛c7+	♔a6
37	♛c8+	♔a5
38	♛c7+	♔b4??

Time-trouble. 37 ... ♔a6 leads to a draw by perpetual check.

| 39 | a3+ | ♔c5 |

If 39 ... ♔xb3 40 ♘d4+ forks

king and queen.

| 40 | ♕xa7+ | ♔xd6 |
| 41 | ♖d1+ *(43)* | |

Black must now give up his queen as it is lost anyway, but only for a knight, after 41 ... ♔e6 42 ♘d4+, while 41 ... ♔e5?? leads to mate after 42 ♕e7+.

41	...	♕d3
42	♖xd3+	♖xd3
43	♕b8+	♔e7
44	♕xh2	♖xb3
45	♕e5+	♔f8
46	♘d4	♖b1+
47	♔d2	♗d7
48	♕d6+	♔e8
49	♘xc6	♗xc6
50	♕xc6+	♔f8
51	♔c2	♖e1
52	♕xb5	♖xe4
53	a4	1-0

This game "tipped over" twice as a result of the mistakes on moves 20 and 38, but from the point of view of opening theory it was convincing enough.

A22

5	...	d6
6	ed	♗xd6
7	♘f3	♘c6
8	♘c3	♗e6
9	h3	♘ge5

Christofferson-Stahlberg, Sweden 1928. White now continued 10 ♘xe5 and after 10 ... ♘xe5 11 ♗e3 ♘xc4 (11 ... ♗xc4?? 12 ♗xc4 ♘xc4 13 ♕a4+) 12 ♗xc4 ♗xc4 13 ♕d4 ♗e6 14 ♕xg7 ♔d7 15 0-0-0 stood clearly better.

Summary

4 ... h5 is not a good continuation. Both 5 h3 and 5 ♗e2 give White the advantage.

More complicated is 4 ... d6 which is the theme of the next two sections.

B

| 4 | ... | d6 |
| 5 | ed | ♗xd6 *(44)* |

| 6 | ♗e2 | |

With superficial moves White

can get a disadvantage, e.g. 6 ♘f3? ♗c5! 7 ♕xd8+ ♔xd8, when Black regains the pawn and stands better.

6 ... f5

The alternative is 6 ... ♘f6. Rishkin-Kazantsev, USSR 1954, continued 7 ♘c3 0-0 8 ♘f3 ♗b4 9 ♕c2 ♗xc3+ 10 bc ♖e8 11 e5 ♘g4 12 ♗f4 ♘c6 13 ♖d1 ♕e7 14 ♖d5 ♗e6 15 h3! ♘h6 (15 ... ♗xd5?? 16 hg threatening ♕xh7+ and ♕h8 mate; 15 ... ♘gxe5 16 ♖xe5 with great advantage for White) 16 0-0! ♗xd5? (a mistake in the worse position) 17 cd ♘a5 18 ♘g5 g6 19 ♘e4 ♔g7 20 ♗g5 ♕d7 21 ♕d2 ♘g8 (21 ... ♘f5 22 ♗f6+ and g4) 22 ♘f6 1-0. Black has no good defence to the mating attack ♘xg8, ♗f6+ and ♕h6.

7 ef ♕e7

The starting point of two important games.

Game 13
Capablanca-Tartakower
Bad Kissingen 1928

(1 d4 ♘f6 2 c4 e5 3 de ♘g4 4 e4 d6 5 ed ♗xd6 6 ♗e2 f5 7 ef ♕e7)

Jose Raoul Capablanca, World Champion 1921-27, was famous, above all, for his fantastic technique in simple positions. He liked to avoid unclear complications. Here there was the opportunity, admittedly at the cost of the opponent's initiative, to win a piece: 8 c5 ♗xc5 9 ♕a4+ ♘c6 10 ♕xg4.

We will see the consequences of this piece sacrifice in the next game. In this game Capablanca continued quietly:

8	♘f3	♗xf5
9	♗g5	♘f6
10	♘c3	♘c6
11	♘d5	♕f7
12	0-0	0-0-0
13	♘d4	♘xd4
14	♕xd4	c6?

Better was 14 ... c5 15 ♕h4 ♘xd5 16 cd (16 ♗xd8? ♘f4!) 16 ... ♖de8 as given by Euwe in his book on Capablanca.

15 ♗xf6 gf (45)

In the above-mentioned work Euwe now gives 16 ♕xa7! cd 17 cd with the possibilities:

a) **17 ... ♕xd5** 18 ♖fd1 ♕e5 19 ♖ac1+ ♔d7 20 ♕xb7+ ♔e8 21 ♗h5+ wins.

b) **17 ... ♗b8** 18 ♖ac1+ ♔d7 19 ♕e3 ♖c8 20 ♗b5+ ♔d8 21 ♕b6+ ♗c7 22 ♖xc7 and wins (22 ... ♖xc7 23 d6; 22 ... ♕xc7 23 ♕xf6+).

c) **17 ... ♔d7** 18 ♖fe1 ♕xd5 19 ♗f3 ♕b5 20 ♗xb7 again winning.

45
W

16 ♕xf6?

Now Black could save himself by 16 ... ♗g6! 17 ♕xg6 (but not 17 ♘e7+ ♗xe7 18 ♕xe7 ♖he8) 17 ... hg 18 ♘e3 ♗xh2+ 19 ♔h1 ♗f4+ 20 ♔g1 ♗h2+ and draws by perpetual check – Euwe. To his misfortune Black missed this possibility.

16	...	♕xf6
17	♘xf6	♗e5
18	♗g4	♗xf6

Better was 18 ... ♗xg4 19 ♘xg4 ♗xb2 20 ♖ab1 ♗d4 (Euwe and Tartakower). White must still lose some tempi (h3, ♔h2) before he can become active with f4.

19	♗xf5+	♔c7
20	♖ad1	♗xb2
21	♖xd8	♖xd8

If 21 ... ♔xd8 22 ♖b1 and 23 ♖xb7.

22	♗xh7	♖d4
23	g3	♖xc4
24	h4	b5

The pawn race begins. Naturally, with an extra pawn and a freer run for his passed pawns, White holds the better hand. The endgame artist Capablanca once again plays the rest of the game magnificently.

25	♔g2	a5
26	h5	♗g7
27	f4	♗h6

Clearly directed against g4.

28	♖e1	♖a4
29	♗g8	♖d4
30	♖e7+	♖d7
31	♖xd7+	♔xd7

32	♔f3	c5
33	g4	c4
34	g5	♗f8
35	h6	a4

If 35 ... c3 36 ♗b3 stops the pawn.

36	f5	♔c6

Or 36 ... c3 37 ♔e2 b4 38 h7 ♗g7 39 f6 ♗h8 40 ♔d3.

37	h7	♗g7
38	f6	♗h8
39	f7	

1-0

While the end of the game was a clear success for White, the opening was not particularly so if we remember the possible improvements for Black on move 15 (... c5).

Three years after this game the critical position on the 7th move occurred again in practice. But this time it was not two such famous names as Capablanca and Tartakower at work, but two little known correspondence players.

Thus it happened that this game almost remained unnoticed by the chess world; in large reference works such as *ECO* it is not even mentioned, let alone analysed. The American Josef Staker, whose booklet on the Budapest Gambit is often quoted in this book, has dug it up from somewhere.

Game 14
Egli-Bauer
Correspondence 1931

(1 d4 ♘f6 2 c4 e5 3 de ♘g4 4 e4 d6

5 ed ♗xd6 6 ♗e2 f5 7 ef ♕e7)

This time the critical piece sacrifice is put to a severe test.

8	c5!	♗xc5
9	♕a4+	♘c6
10	♕xg4	*(46)*

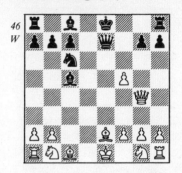

10 ... ♘d4?

This loses quickly, but others are no better:

a) 10 ... ♗xf5 (in *ECO* this is incorrectly given an exclamation mark, attributed to Tartakower) 11 ♕xf5 ♖f8. Now a retreat of the white queen gives Black a raging attack after ... ♗xf2+ and ... ♖d8+ but 12 ♗g5! (Staker) puts an end to Black's hopes:

a1) 12 ... ♕d6 13 ♕e4+
a11) 13 ... ♔d7 14 ♗g4+
a12) 13 ... ♔f7 14 ♗c4+
a13) 13 ... ♘e7 14 ♕xe7+
a14) 13 ... ♘e5 14 ♘f3

a2) 12 ... ♖xf5 13 ♗xe7 ♗xf2+ 14 ♔f1 ♔xe7 15 ♘f3 and White must win with careful play.

a3) 12 ... ♗xf2+ 13 ♕xf2 ♕b4+ (13 ... ♕xg5 14 ♘f3 ♕c1+ 15 ♗d1

followed by 0-0) 14 ♗d2 ♕xb2 15 ♕e3+ and wins.

b) 10 ... 0-0! 11 ♕c4+ ♔h8 12 ♘f3 ♖xf5 13 0-0 b5 14 ♕xb5 ♘b4. So far this is analysis by the Hungarian correspondence master Dr Balogh, who continues incorrectly here 15 ♗d3 c6 16 ♕c4 ♖xf3 17 gf ♗a6 with advantage to Black. Correct is 15 ♘c3! ♗a6 16 ♕xa6 ♘xa6 17 ♗xa6 with advantage to White who has three pieces and a pawn for the queen and can easily consolidate his position with ♗b7 followed by ♗e4.

11 ♕h5+! ♔d7

Other possibilities give no prospects of success:

a) 11 ... g6 12 fg! ♘c2+ 13 ♔d1 ♘xa1 14 g7+ etc.
b) 11 ... ♔d8?? 12 ♗g5 or 11 ... ♕f7 12 ♕xf7+ ♔xf7 13 ♗d1 is not worth discussing.
c) 11 ... ♔f8 12 f6! gf 13 ♗h6+ ♔g8 14 ♘c3! ♘c2+ 15 ♔d1 ♘xa1 16 ♗c4+ ♗e6 17 ♕xc5!! (17 ... ♕xc5 18 ♗xe6 mate) is the prettiest variation of Dr Balogh's given in Staker's booklet.

12	♗g5	♕e5
13	♘c3	♘c2+
14	♔f1	♘xa1
15	♕f7+	♔c6

Or 15 ... ♗e7 16 ♘f3 ♕d6 17 ♘e4 ♕b4 18 ♘e5+ ♔d8 19 ♘d3 and wins.

16 ♗f3+ ♔b6

Or 16 ... ♔d6 17 ♘b5 mate.

17 ♗f4 1-0

If the black queen moves White mates on c7. 17 ... ♕xf4 (♕e7) 18 ♘d5+ wins the queen.

This is all well and good, but such complicated variations are not to everyone's taste. For this reason White sometimes forgoes taking on d6 and continues his development. This is the theme of C.

C

| 4 | ... | d6 |
| 5 | ♗e2 *(47)* | |

In this way White avoids all the complications of B. The game is conducted on quiet, positional lines.

Black can play 5 ... h5 which leads to a position already examined in A (see game 12).

| 5 | ... | ♘xe5 |
| 6 | f4 | |

Black has three knight moves at his disposal:
C1 6 ... ♘ec6
C2 6 ... ♘g6
C3 6 ... ♘g4

C1

| 6 | ... | ♘ec6 |
| 7 | ♘f3 | ♗g4 |

8 0-0 ♗e7 9 ♘c3 ♘d7 10 h3 ♗xf3 11 ♗xf3 0-0 12 ♗e3 ♘b6 13 b3 ♗f6 14 ♕d2 ♘e7 15 ♖ad1 with advantage to White, Ulvestad-Haro, Malaga 1965.

C2

| 6 | ... | ♘g6 |
| 7 | ♘f3 | ♘c6 |

8 0-0 ♗e7 9 ♘c3 0-0 10 ♗e3 ♖e8 11 ♕d2 ♗f6 12 ♘d4 ♗d7 13 ♖ae1 ♘xd4 14 ♗xd4 ♗c6 15 ♗d1, Katajisto-de Greiff, Amsterdam Ol 1954, and after manoeuvring the bishop to c2 White had a permanent plus due to his overwhelming space advantage.

Both these examples are given in *ECO* by IM Minev.

C3

| 6 | ... | ♘g4 |

A try of the American Mayers who has been much involved in the Budapest Gambit and who publishes his analysis in his own occasional bulletins.

The knight on g4 is indirectly protected: 7 ♗xg4 ♕h4+ 8 g3 ♕xg4 and Black stands well.

White must play differently:

| 7 | ♘f3 |

Now:
C31 7 ... ♗e7
C32 7 ... ♘c6

C31

| 7 | ... | &e7 |

Mayers was mainly concerned with the combination 8 0-0 d5!? 9 ed &c5+. Even here everything is not clear, but it remains an academic question as White can get an advantage by simple means.

| 8 | ♘c3! | 0-0 |
| 9 | 0-0 | ♘c6 |

Here 9 ... d5 is completely wrong: 10 ♕xd5 ♕xd5 11 ♘xd5 &c5+ 12 ♔h1 and ... ♘f2+ is excluded because of the threat ♘xc7. If Black had played 8 ... ♘c6 instead of castling, Mayers' idea is still not feasible: 8 ... ♘c6 9 0-0 d5 10 cd &c5+ 11 ♔h1 ♘e7 (11 ... ♘f2+?? 12 ♖xf2 and dc) 12 ♕e1 and White is simply two pawns up.

| 10 | h3 | ♘f6 |

11 &e3 ♖e8 12 ♘d4 &f8 13 &f3 &d7 14 ♖c1 ♘xd4 15 &xd4 &c6 16 ♕d3 g6 17 ♖fd1 &g7 18 b4 a6 19 a4. White has a big space advantage.

C32

7	...	♘c6
8	0-0	&d7
9	♘c3	&e7
10	h3	♘f6
11	e5	de
12	fe	♘g8

12 ... ♘h5? 13 ♔h2! followed by g4.

| 13 | &e3 | f6 |
| 14 | &d3! | *(48)* |

48
B

Black has a very poor position, Reshevsky-Denker, Syracuse 1934. There is nothing to be done about the simple White plan ♕c2 and ♖ae1 or ♖ad1. Furthermore, 14 ... ♘xe5?? fails to 15 ♘xe5 fe 16 ♕h5+ g6 17 ♕xg6+! hg 18 &xg6 mate. Equally horrible for Black is 14 ... fe 15 ♘xe5 ♘f6 (15 ... ♘xe5 16 ♕h5+ g6 17 ♕xe5 ♘f6 18 ♖xf6) 16 ♖xf6! &xf6 17 ♕h5+ g6 18 &xg6+ and you can find the rest for yourself.

Summary

In the variation 4 ... d6 a sharp struggle arises after accepting the pawn (B). Although White has advantages, he is running a few risks. Declining the gambit with 5 &e2 (C) assures White a clear space advantage without any problems.

It is advisable for Black to play 4 ... ♘xe5 immediately after 4 e4. In those variations (the theme of the last two sections of this chapter) Black has the best prospects of satisfactory counterplay.

D

4	...	♘xe5
5	f4	♘g6 *(49)*

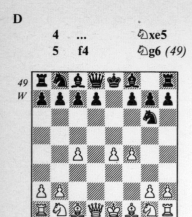

The advantage of this move is that the pawn on f4 comes under fire. What can prove a disadvantage is that White always has f5 at his disposal. This advance cannot be made now (and usually not in the next few moves) as Black would then gladly put his knight on e5, the classic square of operations in the Budapest Gambit.

White must therefore first fight to control this square.

D1 6 ♘f3

D2 6 ♗e3

First we look at some sidelines:
a) **6 ♘c3 ♗b4 7 ♗e3** transposes to D2. The alternative is 7 ♗d2 ♗xc3 8 ♗xc3 ♘xf4 9 ♗xg7 ♖g8 10 ♗c3 ♘xg2+ 11 ♗xg2 ♖xg2 with a sharp position in which White hardly has compensation for the lost pawn.

b) **6 a3** and now Black can equalise easily with 6 ... a5 followed by ...

♘a6 and ... ♗c5 – Tartakower. For those who like sharp positions here is the analysis from *ECO* and Staker: 6 ... ♗c5 7 ♘f3 (7 b4 ♗xg1 8 ♖xg1 0-0 9 ♕f3 d6 10 g4 a5 11 b5 ♘d7 12 ♖a2 ♘c5 13 ♗e3 b6 with positional advantage for Black, Mechkarov-Atanasov, corres 1955) 7 ... d6 8 b4 ♗b6 9 f5 ♘h4 10 ♘g5 ♕e7 11 c5 dc 12 ♗c4 cb *(50)*

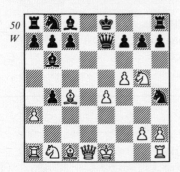

Mechkarov mentions 13 ♗xf7+ ♔f8 with better chances for Black.

Staker gives 13 ♕h5 ♘xf5 14 ♕xf7+ ♕xf7 15 ♗xf7+ ♔e7 16 ef h6 17 ♗g6 as won for White (17 ... hg 18 ♗xg5+ with an attack) but overlooks the simple 17 ... ♗d4!, e.g. 18 ♖a2 hg 19 ♗xg5+ ♗f6 20 ♖e2+ ♔d8 21 ♗xf6+ gf 22 ♖d2+ ♘d7 23 ab c6 and Black, with a strong knight posted on e5 has a satisfactory game (his plan is 24 ... ♔c7 and 25 ... ♘e5, to be followed by ... a5).

D1

6	♘f3 *(51)*

Threatens f5. Black's best continuation is 6 ... ♗b4+. With reference to 6 ... ♗c5 see the following famous game.

Game 15
Alekhine–Seitz
Baden-Baden 1925

(1 d4 ♘f6 2 c4 e5 3 de ♘g4 4 e4 ♘xe5 5 f4 ♘g6)

6	♘f3	♗c5?
7	f5!	♘h4?

Relatively better was 7 ... ♘e7 but not 7 ... ♘e5 8 ♘xe5 ♕h4+ 9 g3 ♕xe4+ 10 ♗e2 ♕xh1 11 ♘g6+ and wins.

The text sets a simple trap (8 ♗g5?? ♘xf3+) but after the strong reply

| 8 | ♘g5! | |

Black's disadvantage is already decisive. The knight on h4 is cut off and 8 ... h6 is refuted by 9 ♘xf7 ♔xf7 10 ♕d5+ etc.

| 8 | ... | ♕e7 |
| 9 | ♕g4 | f6 |

Clearly the only move.

| 10 | ♕h5+! | g6 |

Or 10 ... ♔f8 11 ♕xh4! (but not 11 ♘xh7+? ♔g8!) 11 ... fg 12 ♗xg5 with enormous advantage to White.

11	♕xh4	fg
12	♗xg5	♕f7
13	♗e2	0-0
14	♖f1	♘c6
15	♘c3	♘d4
16	fg	♕xg6
17	♖xf8+	♗xf8
18	♗h5	♕b6 (52)

Black fights ingeniously in a lost position. After the plausible 19 ♕f2 (protecting b2 and also threatening mate by ♕f7+ and ♕xf8), Black counters with 19 ... ♘c2+!! (20 ♕xc2 ♕g1+ 21 ♔e2 ♕xg2+ and ... ♕xg5) and quite unexpectedly survives.

19	0-0-0!	♗g7
20	♖f1	♘e6
21	♗f7+	♔h8
22	♗xe6	♕xe6
23	♗f6!	
	1-0	

White wins in every variation,

e.g. 23 ... ♗xf6 24 ♖xf6 ♕e8 25 ♕h6 ♔g8 26 ♘d5 or 23 ... d6 24 ♗xg7+ ♔xg7 25 ♕g5+ ♕g6 26 ♕e7+ ♔h6 27 ♖f6.

As we have just seen so vividly, 6 ♘f3 threatens f5 immediately. Therefore Black must not delay (6 ... ♗c5?) but check immediately.

6   ...   ♗b4+ *(53)*

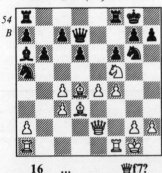

53
W

Now the main continuation is 7 ♘c3 (see game 16). White also has:

a) **7 ♘bd2??** ♘xf4 with advantage.

b) **7 ♗d2** ♕e7 (threatening both ... ♘xf4 and ... ♕e4+) 8 ♔f2 ♗xd2 (8 ... ♗c5+? 9 ♔g3!) 9 ♕xd2 ♕xe4 10 ♗d3 (10 g3 0-0) 10 ... ♕xf4 11 ♖e1+ ♔d8. This variation is untested but the author can see no compensation for the two sacrificed pawns, e.g. 12 ♕c3 ♕f6 13 ♕c2 d6 14 ♘c3 ♗e6 etc.

c) **7 ♔f2** ♗c5+ 8 ♔g3 (8 ♗e3 ♗xe3+ 9 ♔xe3 ♕f6!) 8 ... d6 9 a3 a5 with about equal chances. White must still lose two tempi to hide his king by h3 and ♔h2. The ending after 10 f5 ♘e5 11 ♘xe5 de

12 ♕xd8+ ♔xd8 followed by ... c6 is rather in Black's favour due to the hole on d4.

Game 16
Chebotayev-Isayev
USSR 1948

(1 d4 ♘f6 2 c4 e5 3 de ♘g4 4 e4 ♘xe5 5 f4 ♘g6 6 ♘f3 ♗b4+)

7   ♘c3   0-0

We will look at the alternatives 7 ... d6 and 7 ... ♕f6 later.

8	**♗d3**	**d6**
9	**0-0**	**♗xc3**
10	**bc**	**♘c6**
11	**♕c2**	**b6**
12	**♘d4**	**♘a5**
13	**♗e3**	**♕d7**

13 ... ♗a6 14 ♕e2 could transpose to the game.

14	**♘f5**	**♗a6**
15	**♗d4**	**f6**
16	**♕e2** *(54)*	

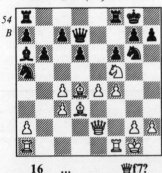

54
B

16   ...   ♕f7?

Black takes aim at the pawn on c4 much too early. He should have played 16 ... ♖ae8. After 17 ♖f3, for example, (with the idea ♖h3 and ♕h5) an exchange sacrifice comes into consideration: 17 ... ♕xf5 18 ef ♖xe2 19 ♗xe2 ♘h4 20 ♖f2 ♘xf5 and Black still catches the c4 pawn. After 16 ... ♖ae8 17 ♖ae1 ♕f7 Black's chances would be much better than in the game.

17 e5! ♖ae8

Or 17 ... ♗xc4 18 ef ♗xd3 19 ♕xd3 winning the pawn on g7, as 19 ... gf?? loses to 20 ♘h6+. Furthermore, 17 ... fe? 18 fe doesn't help as ♘h6+ is again threatened and the rook on f1 enters the fray.

18 ♕g4 fe
19 fe ♕e6

19 ... ♘xe5?? 20 ♘h6+.

20 ed ♗xc4
21 ♗xc4 ♘xc4

White now wins with an energetic attack in which the pawn on d6 plays a key role.

22 ♘h6+! gh

Black has no choice: 22 ... ♔h8 23 ♕xe6 ♖xe6 24 ♘f7+ ♔g8 25 d7! wins.

23 ♖xf8+ ♔xf8
24 ♖f1+ ♔g8 (55)

25 d7! ♕e7
26 de♕+ ♕xe8
27 ♕f3 1-0

The threats ♕d5+ and ♕f6 cannot both be parried. Black's defeat was not absolutely due to the opening. 7 ... 0-0 must be examined more closely. On his 7th move Black has other possibilities:

7 ♘c3 (56)

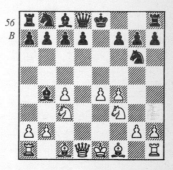

a) **7 ... ♕f6** 8 e5 ♕b6 9 f5 ♘e7 10 ♗d3 d5!? (but not 10 ... ♗xc3+ 11 bc d6 12 f6 with advantage to White – Staker) with an unclear position after 11 f6 d4 or 11 ed ♘xf5.

b) **7 ... d6** 8 ♗d3 ♗c5 9 ♘a4! and White is a bit better, e.g. 9 ... ♗b4+ 10 ♔f2! followed by a3, or 9 ... ♘c6 10 ♘xc5 dc 11 ♗e3 with some advantage to White according to Mechkarov. Instead of 8 ... ♗c5 the following moves çan be considered:

b1) **8 ... 0-0** transposing to game 16.

b2) **8 ... a6** 9 0-0 ♗c5+ 10 ♔h1
♘c6

b3) **8 ... ♗xc3+** 9 bc ♕f6 10 ♕d2
♘d7 followed by ... ♘c5.

D2

6   ♗e3 *(57)*

White prevents 6 ... ♗c5.

6   ...   ♗b4+

7   ♘c3

7 ♘d2 is not good on account of
7 ... ♕e7 8 ♕c2 (the natural
protection 8 ♗d3 fails here to 8 ...
♕d6! with a surprising win of a
pawn – Steiner) 8 ... ♘c6 9 ♘gf3
b6 with a good game for Black –
Grünfeld, e.g. 10 a3 ♗c5 $\overline{\overline{\mp}}$; 10
♗d3 ♗c5 11 ♘xc5 ♕xc5 12 g3
♕e3+ $\overline{\overline{\mp}}$; 10 g3 ♗b7 11 ♗g2 ♗c5 =.

7   ...   ♗xc3+

8   bc   b6!?

An interesting alternative to the
possible variation 8 ... ♕e7 9 ♗d3
f5 10 ♕c2 fe 11 ♗xe4 ♘xf4 12
♗xf4 d5 13 cd ♗f5 winning back
the piece in a game Meier-Grünfeld.

9   ♗d3

9 ♕d5? ♘c6 and White's queen
is soon exposed.

9   ...   ♗b7

10   ♘f3   d6

11   0-0   ♘d7

with level chances. White can never
play f5 because of the square e5. If
White does nothing active, there
follows ... 0-0, ... ♖e8 and ... ♘c5
with pressure against White's centre.
Heim-Schröder, 1967, continued
sharply 12 e5 de 13 ♗xg6 (13 fe?
♗xf3 14 ♕xf3 ♘dxe5) 13 ... hg 14
fe ♕e7 15 ♗g5 ♕c5+ 16 ♕d4 ♘f8
17 ♕xc5 bc 18 ♖ab1 ♗a6 19 ♘d2
♘e6 20 ♗f4 (20 ♗e3 ♖h5) 20
... 0-0-0 21 ♖b2 ♖d3 and Black
went on to win. The rest of the
game is unfortunately unavailable,
but there is no doubting Black's
advantage.

This game fragment does not
provide enough evidence to make
a correct assessment of 8 ... b6, but
this plan certainly deserves further
investigation. If it does not hold
good, Black still has the example
Meier-Grünfeld (see note to Black's
8th) to fall back on.

Summary

5 ... ♘g6 is probably playable.
Black has more problems in the
variation 6 ♘f3. In both variations
(6 ♘f3 and 6 ♗e3) Black *must* play
6 ... ♗b4+.

In the opinion of the Swedish
IMs and Budapest experts Harry

Schüssler and Tom Wedberg, Black has an easier task if he decides on 5 ... ♘ec6. This is the subject of the last section of the Alekhine system.

E

4	...	♘xe5
5	f4	♘ec6 (58)

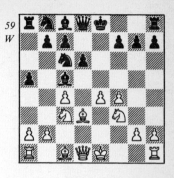

Here the black knight is not exposed. Furthermore, black holes have appeared in White's camp (particularly d4). In our first illustrative game the Soviet GM overlooked this hole and only narrowly avoided defeat.

Game 17
Vaganian-Wedberg
Buenos Aires Ol 1978

(1 d4 ♘f6 2 c4 e5 3 de ♘g4 4 e4 ♘xe5 5 f4 ♘ec6)

6	♘f3	♗c5
7	♘c3	d6
8	♗d3	a5 (59)

A multi-purpose move. It controls b4 (countering an eventual a3 and b4) and the bishop on c5

can settle on a7 if necessary (e.g. after ♘a4).

9	h3

White does something about ... ♗g4. IM Minev does not like 9 h3 and cites the following variation: 9 ♕e2 ♗g4 10 ♗e3 ♘d4 11 ♕f2 ♗xf3 12 ♗xd4! with advantage to White (Wedberg). However, instead of 11 ... ♗xf3?, 11 ... ♘e6!? comes strongly into consideration (12 h3? ♘xf4!; 12 0-0? ♘xf4!; 12 ♗xc5 dc!? threatening the bishop on d3 and the pawn on f4). Also after 12 g3 ♘c6 Black has a satisfactory game. It was probably just this variation that White wanted to avoid and therefore played 9 h3.

9	...	♘a6
10	♘d5	♗e6
11	a3	

11 ♗e3 ♗xd5! 12 ♗xc5 ♗xe4 with advantage to Black – Wedberg.

11	...	0-0

How should White get castled? 12 ♗e3 is again refuted by 12 ... ♗xd5 and the preparatory 12 ♕e2

(still to play ♗e3) is answered by
12 ... ♖e8 after which White is in
danger on the e-file (13 ♗e3 f5! 14
0-0 ♗xd5 15 cd fe wins).

12	f5	♗xd5
13	cd	♘e5
14	♘xe5?!	

Relatively better was 14 ♗f4
(Wedberg) though Black still stands
somewhat better: 14 ... ♘xf3+ 15
♕xf3 ♗d4 16 0-0-0 ♕f6 17 ♖d2
g5! with a dark-squared blockade
and use of e5 (Plan: ... ♘c5-d7).

14	...	♕h4+
15	♔d2	de
16	♔c2	♗d4
17	♖f1	c6
18	d6	

If 18 dc ♖fc8 with an attack.

18	...	♘c5
19	f6	♖fd8
20	fg *(60)*	

60
B

| 20 | ... | ♖xd6? |

Correct now was 20 ... ♘xd3! 21
♕xd3 (21 ♕f3? ♘f2! wins) 21 ...
♖xd6 with great, if not already
decisive, advantage for Black, e.g.

22 ♗d2 (with the trap 22 ... ♗xb2??
23 ♕f3) 22 ... ♕e7 23 ♕f3 f6
followed by ... ♕xg7, ... ♔h8 and
... ♖g8. Black would then have a
healthy extra pawn, a dominating
bishop on d4 and pressure on the
g- and d-files, while White cannot
do much on the f-file.

| 21 | ♕f3 | ♖d7 |

Or 21 ... ♕e7 22 ♗c4!. Black
should have taken this resuscitated
bishop earlier.

| 22 | g3! | ♕e7 |

But not 22 ... ♕xh3?? 23 ♗c4!
(threatening to trap the queen by
♖h1) 23 ... ♖e7 24 ♖h1 ♕d7 25
♕h5 and White wins.

| 23 | ♗c4 | ♘xe4! |
| 24 | ♗d3! | |

The only move. 24 ♕xe4 ♘c5 25
♕e2 b5 leads to the loss of the
attacking bishop and Black is running matters again.

| 24 | ... | ♘g5 |

Intending to refute the sally 25
♕h5 by 25 ... e4! (26 ♗xg5 ed+ 27
♔b1 ♕e6 etc).

25	♗xg5	♕xg5
26	h4	♕xg7
27	♖ae1	♔h8
28	♖e4	♖g8
29	♕f5	

Now 29 ... ♖e7 30 ♖g4! ♕h6!
was indicated (Wedberg) and Black
could still have played for a win.
In time trouble he committed a
grave error.

| 29 | ... | ♖d6?? |

30	♕xf7	♕xf7
31	♖xf7	♖g7
32	♖f8+	♖g8
33	♖f7	

½-½

33 ... ♖h6 34 ♖xb7 ♖xg3 35 ♗c4 (if 35 ... ♖h5?? 36 ♖g4; but on the other hand White threatens ♖b8+ followed by ♖g8+ and ♖xg3) so Wedberg opted to repeat moves.

Summary

Black stood well out of the opening. 6 ♘f3 allowing 6 ... ♗c5 is not so good as White has problems with castling. It is natural to prevent 6 ... ♗c5 by 6 ♗e3 and this is the main variation of this section. First we will look briefly at another apparently harmless, but really quite dangerous, move.

E1

6   a3!? *(61)*

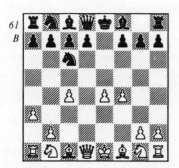

A trap. After 6 ... ♗c5?! 7 b4! ♗xg1 8 ♖xg1 ♕h4+ (relatively

better is 8 ... 0-0 but then Black has no compensation for the loss of the bishop pair) 9 g3 ♕xh2 10 ♖g2 ♕h1 11 ♗b2 White has powerful compensation for the sacrificed pawn.

| 6 | ... | a5 |
| 7 | ♗e3 | ♘a6 |

Black follows the typical dark-squared strategy of the Budapest Gambit and wants to exchange the bishop on e3. White can hardly prevent this, e.g. 8 ♕d5? b6 9 ♘f3 ♗b7 10 ♗d3 ♘c5! and Black stands clearly better (11 ♗c2 ♘b4 12 ♕d2 ♘xc2+ 13 ♕xc2 ♗xe4; 11 ♗xc5 ♗xc5). The queen move to d5, as almost always in this gambit, does not work out well.

| 8 | ♘c3 | ♗c5 |
| 9 | ♕d2 | |

Worse is 9 ♗xc5 ♘xc5 as Black can later fix the hole on b3 by ... a4.

9	...	d6
10	♘f3	0-0
11	♗d3	♖e8 *(62)*

with a roughly equal game, e.g. 12 0-0 ♗xe3+ 13 ♕xe3 ♘c5 14 ♗c2 a4 15 ♖ae1 ♗e6! (15 ... f6?! 16 ♕f2 ♗g4 17 ♘d4 ♕d7 18 ♘d5 wins – Kmoch) 16 ♘d5 (16 ♕e2 ♘a5!) 16 ... ♘a5 with complicated play, e.g. 17 ♕c3 f6 18 ♘d4 ♗f7 followed by 19 ... c6. The attack 19 ♘f5 c6 20 ♕g3 is easily parried by 20 ... ♗g6.

Summary

Black's counterplay in this variation is based on the weaknesses b3 and c4 in White's position, brought about by the premature advance a2-a3. We now pass on to the main variation which forgoes interpolating the moves 6 a3 a5.

E2

6 ♗e3 (63)

White prevents the development of the enemy bishop on c5, so another square presents itself.

6 ... ♗b4+

7 ♘c3

White has two other significant possibilities:

a) **7 ♔f2** ♘a6 8 a3 (8 ♘c3 ♗xc3 9 bc leads to the main variation with the 'gift' tempo ♔f2) 8 ... ♗c5 and now:

a1) **9 b4?** ♕f6! wins material.

a2) **9 ♗xc5** ♘xc5 10 ♕c2 ♕f6 is in Black's favour.

a3) **9 ♕d2** ♕f6 10 g3 ♗xe3+ 11 ♔xe3 ♘c5 12 ♕c3 ♕e7 13 ♗g2 0-0 is good for Black on account of the bad position of the white king. Black plans 14 ... a5 and if 14 b4 then 14 ... ♘e6 followed by ... a5!.

b) **7 ♘d2** ♕h4+ 8 g3 ♕e7 and here *ECO* quotes two practical examples:

b1) **9 ♗g2** a5 10 ♘e2 ♘a6 11 0-0 d6 12 ♘b3 ♗g4 13 h3 ♗xe2 14 ♕xe2 a4 was Pomar-Heidenfeld, Enschede 1963.

b2) **9 ♕f3** ♘a6 10 0-0-0 ♘c5 11 ♗xc5 ♗xc5 12 ♘b3 d6 13 ♘e2 f5 14 ♘xc5 dc 15 e5 0-0 (followed by ... ♗e6 and ... ♖ad8) Visier-O'Kelly, Malaga 1967, with equality in both cases.

We now examine the following variations in examples from tournament practice:

E21 7 ... d6
E22 7 ... ♕e7
E23 7 ... ♕h4+

Game 18
Chebotayev-Machkin
USSR 1968

(1 d4 ♘f6 2 c4 e5 3 de ♘g4 4 e4 ♘xe5 5 f4 ♘ec6 6 ♗e3 ♗b4+)

7	♘c3	d6
8	♕c2	♘a6
9	0-0-0	♗g4
10	♗e2	♗xe2
11	♘gxe2	♕c8
12	♘g3	♗c5
13	♗xc5	♘xc5
14	e5	de
15	♘f5	♘e6
16	fe	♘xe5?

Too optimistic. 16 ... 0-0 was indicated, followed by ... ♕e8 and ... ♖d8. Black certainly has a passive position here.

17	♖he1	f6
18	♘e4	

By grabbing the pawn on e5 Black has forfeited the possibility of castling – e7 is not protected.

18	...	♔f8
19	♕f2	♘f7
20	♘c5	♘xc5
21	♕xc5+	♘d6
22	♖xd6!	cd
23	♕xd6+	♔f7
24	♕e7+	♔g6
25	♕xg7+	♔xf5
26	g4+	♔f4
27	♕xf6+	
	1-0	

The set-up with 7 ... d6 brought Black quite a passive position, mainly because this move does nothing about White's centre. In the next game Black immediately exerts pressure against the white pawn on e4.

Game 19
Alekhine-Seitz
Hastings 1925-26

(1 d4 ♘f6 2 c4 e5 3 de ♘g4 4 e4 ♘xe5 5 f4 ♘ec6 6 ♗e3 ♗b4+)

7	♘c3	♕e7 (64)

In comparison with game 18, Black reacts much better here, immediately eyeing the pawn on e4.

8	♗d3?	f5?

But not like this! A rule of thumb: *pressure on the e-pawn must be conducted with pieces!* Better was 8 ... ♗xc3+ 9 bc ♘a6 10 ♕f3 ♘c5 11 ♗c2 b6 followed by ... ♗b7 and ... 0-0-0. We will see a similar idea in improved form in the next game.

9	♕h5+!	

A far-sighted manoeuvre. The a1-h8 diagonal is weakened by the forced ... g6 and the bishop on e3 will subsequently do great deeds there (see Alekhine's note to Black's 16th move).

9	...	g6
10	♕f3	♗xc3+
11	bc	fe?

Somewhat better was 11 ... d6 though White still has more of the game after 12 ♘e2 0-0 13 ♘g3 ♘a6 14 0-0 ♗d7 15 ♖ab1.

12	♗xe4	0-0
13	♗d5+	♔h8
14	♘h3	d6
15	0-0	♗xh3
16	♕xh3	♕d7

Alekhine gives the following variation: 16 ... ♘d7 17 ♖ae1 ♕g7 18 f5 g5 19 ♖b1 ♖ab8 20 f6 ♘xf6 21 ♗xc6 bc 22 ♖xb8 ♖xb8 23 ♗d4 ♖f8 24 ♕e6 and wins.

	17	f5! *(65)*

The decisive move. After 17 ... ♖xf5 18 g4! ♖xf1+ 19 ♖xf1 White's attack wins, e.g. 19 ... ♕g7 20 ♗h6; 19 ... ♕e7 20 ♖f7; 19 ... ♘d8 20 ♗d4+ etc.

17	...	gf
18	♖ab1!	

White wants to provoke ... b6 which weakens the position of the knight on c6. This idea is made clear in the following variation given by Kotov: 18 ... b6 19 ♖be1 (threatening 20 ♗h6 followed by 21 ♖xf5) 19 ... ♘a6 20 ♗xc6 ♕xc6 21 ♗d4+ ♔g8 22 ♕g3+ etc.

In a very bad position Black tries to relieve the pressure by exchanging queens.

18	...	f4
19	♗xf4	♕xh3
20	♗e5+!	
	1-0	

If 20 ... ♘xe5 21 ♖xf8+ ♔g7 22 ♖g8+ ♔h6 23 gh wins.

Karl Gilg, a Czechoslovak master of German origin who settled in West Germany after the second World War, tried an interesting improvement in the last game of this section. He was able to equalise convincingly. Though Gilg finally lost this game, one should not forget that his opponent, Paul Keres, was one of the greatest chess personalities of the 20th century.

Game 20
Keres-Gilg
Prague 1937

(1 d4 ♘f6 2 c4 e5 3 de ♘g4 4 e4 ♘xe5 5 f4 ♘ec6 6 ♗e3 ♗b4+)

7	♘c3	♕h4+!

Similar to Alekhine's manoeuvre in the previous game. Here too the queen check is bound to weaken a diagonal and thus increase the effectiveness of the queen's bishop. It is obvious that Black will subsequently develop his bishop on this diagonal at b7.

	8	g3	♗xc3+
	9	bc	♕e7
	10	♗d3	

After 10 ♗g2 Black obtains a satisfactory game with 10 ... b6, e.g. 11 ♘e2 ♗b7 12 0-0 ♘a6 followed by ... 0-0-0 and ... ♘c5.

	10	...	♘a6
	11	♗c2!	

To answer 11 ... ♘c5 with 12 ♕d5.

	11	...	b6
	12	♘f3	♘c5
	13	0-0!	

The pawn is poisoned: 13 ... ♘xe4? 14 ♗xe4 ♕xe4 15 ♗xb6! followed by ♖e1.

	13	...	♗b7
	14	e5	0-0-0
	15	♘d4	*(66)*

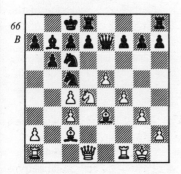

66
B

The game is equal. Black should now have played 15 ... g6! which

makes the square f5 inaccessible to the white knight and prepares something active such as ... f6, ... d6 or ... ♘a5.

The game continuation is risky and White assumes the initiative.

	15	...	f6?
	16	♘f5	♕f8
	17	♗d4	g6
	18	♘e3	fe
	19	fe	♕h6
	20	♘d5	♘e6
	21	♕d3	♖hf8
	22	♖f6	

According to Vasconsellos in "Staker" Black could equalise here with 22 ... ♘cxd4 23 cd ♗xd5 24 ♖xf8 ♖xf8 25 cd ♘g5 26 ♖f1 ♘h3+ 27 ♔g2 ♖xf1 28 ♔xf1. The author cannot agree with this judgement. This ending is better for White who can continue, for example, with ♗b3 and e6.

	22	...	♕h5
	23	♖e1	♘cxd4
	24	cd	♗xd5 *(67)*

67
W

Apparently 22 ... ♕h5 has turned

out all right for Black, e.g. 25 cd
♖xf6 26 ef ♕xd5 or 25 ♖xf8 ♖xf8
26 cd ♘g5. However, there now
follows a surprise:

| 25 | ♗d1! | ♗xc4 |

If Black moves his queen, White
plays ♖xf8 followed by cd. The
square f3, in contrast to the
previous variation, would then be
firmly in White's hands.

26	♕xc4	♕g5
27	♗f3	♔b8
28	♕d5	c6
29	♕d6+	♔b7
30	♖xf8	♖xf8

Or 30 ... ♘xf8 31 e6! ♘xe6 32
♖xe6! wins a piece as 32 ... de
allows 33 ♕xc6+ ♔a6 34 ♕a4
mate.

31	♕xd7+	♘c7
32	♕xc6+	
	1-0	

Despite this loss (to a world-
class player!) Karl Gilg's idea,
now almost fifty years old, still
deserves consideration.

4 Rare Systems

1	d4	♘f6
2	c4	e5
3	de	♘g4

The rare systems are divided into two groups:

A White protects the pawn on e5 by various moves apart from 4 ♘f3 and 4 ♗f4, which were examined in the first two chapters.

B Other moves.

A

White's other means of protecting the pawn on e5 are:

A1 4 f4
A2 4 ♕d4
A3 4 ♕d5

A1

4	f4?	*(68)*

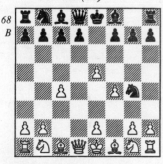

4	...	♗c5

This creates confusion in White's camp. Now 5 e3 ♘xe3 6 ♗xe3 ♗xe3 is clearly better for Black.

5	♘h3	d6
6	ed	cd
7	e4	0-0
8	♘c3	♖e8

Black has splendid play for the sacrificed pawn, e.g. 9 ♗d3 ♕h4+ 10 ♔d2 ♘e3 11 ♕e2 ♗g4 or 9 g3 ♘c6 10 ♗d3 ♕f6 11 ♘d5 (11 ♗d2 ♕h6!) 11 ... ♕h6! and Black wins, e.g. 12 ♘c7 ♕xh3 13 ♘xe8 ♕g2 14 ♖f1 ♘f2 (15 ♕d2 ♗b4; 15 ♕c2 ♘b4; 15 ♕e2 ♗g4; 15 ♕b3 ♘a5 16 ♕c3 ♗b4).

The variation 4 f4? is bad. White loses time and weakens the diagonal g1-a7.

A2

4	♕d4?!	*(69)*

With this move White not only defends the pawn on e5 but at the same time attacks the knight on g4. Therefore 4 ♕d4 does not lack a certain logic; it is interesting to note that this move is played by many chess computers.

However it has one disadvantage: the queen is exposed on d4 and really invites the win of a tempo with ... ♘c6. First, though, something must be done about saving the knight on g4.

Game 21
Laszlo-Abonyi
Budapest 1933

(1 d4 ♘f6 2 c4 e5 3 de ♘g4)

    4   ♕d4   d6

    5   ed

Or 5 ♘f3 ♘c6 comfortably regaining the pawn on e5 with the win of a tempo as the white queen must move.

    5   ...   ♗xd6

Naturally ... ♗b4+ winning the queen is threatened. Snatching another pawn only increases Black's dangerous initiative: 6 ♕e4+ (6 ♕xg7 ♗e5!) 6 ... ♗e6 7 ♕xb7 ♘d7 8 e3 0-0 9 ♘f3 ♘c5 10 ♕b5 ♖b8 11 ♕a5 (or 11 ♕c6 ♖b6) 11 ... ♘d3+ followed by ... ♗b4+ or ... ♘xf2 – 0-1 in a computer

game.

    6   ♘f3   0-0

    7   h3

Black's lead in development is also practically decisive after 7 ♘c3, e.g. 7 ... ♘c6 8 ♕d1 ♗c5 9 e3 ♕xd1+! 10 ♘xd1 ♘b4.

    7   ...   ♘c6

    8   ♕e4

8 ♕d1 is immediately refuted by 8 ... ♘xf2! 9 ♔xf2 ♗g3+ winning the queen.

    8   ...   ♖e8

    9   ♕c2   ♘b4

    10   ♕c3 *(70)*

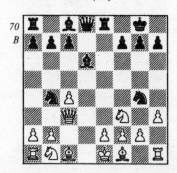

Black has a crushing advantage and could now decide the game with 10 ... ♘d3+! (10 ... ♗f5! also wins) 11 ♕xd3 (11 ♔d2 ♗b4; 11 ♔d1 ♘dxf2+) 11 ... ♗b4+ winning the queen after 12 ♔d1 ♘xf2+ or 12 ♗d2 ♕xd3.

Instead of this he chooses an admittedly effective but less powerful move:

    10   ...   ♘e3?!

The intruder is inviolable as 11

fe?? allows 11 ... ♗g3 mate and 11 ♗xe3 ♖xe3 12 ♕d2 (12 ♕xe3 ♘c2+; 12 fe ♗g3 mate) 12 ... ♘d3+ 13 ♔d1 ♘xf2+ 14 ♔e1 ♘xh1 wins a rook for Black as the rook on e3 is again taboo (15 ♕xe3?? ♗g3+ and mates).

Furthermore 11 ... ♘ec2+ is threatened. Therefore White over-protects c2.

    11   ♘a3   ♘bc2+
    12   ♘xc2   ♗b4 *(71)*

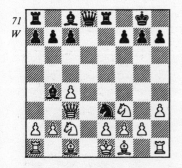

71
W

Naturally this bishop cannot be taken because of ♕d1 mate or ... ♘xc2 mate, but after 13 ♗xe3 ♗xc3+ 14 bc White could still fight. The "great bluff" has worked. Clearly demoralised by a series of unexpected moves **White resigned**.

A real curiosity. As far as the variation 4 ♕d4 is concerned, the final assessment is that it is not very good as the attacks on the white queen considerably enhance Black's development.

A3

    4   ♕d5 *(72)*

72
B

Rapid mobilisation of the queen-side is also the correct method here.

    4   ...   ♘c6
    5   ♘f3

5 f4 ♘b4 6 ♕e4 ♗c5 7 ♘h3 0-0 8 ♘c3 f5 9 ef ♘xf6 10 ♕b1 d5 11 a3 ♘c6 12 cd ♘xd5 13 ♕a2 ♗e6 with advantage to Black – *ECO*.

    5   ...   d6

White now has two possibilities:
A31 6 ♗g5
A32 6 ed

A31

    6   ♗g5   ♗e7
    7   ♗xe7   ♘xe7
    8   ♕e4   de

Black stands well here. 9 ♘xe5? is the 'Schlechter trap' (named after the Austrian grandmaster Carl Schlechter): 9 ... ♕d1+!! 10 ♔xd1 ♘xf2+ with clear advantage for Black.

A32

6	ed	♗e6!
7	d7+ *(73)*	

Or 7 ♕d1 ♗xd6 8 e3 ♕f6 gives Black the advantage – *ECO*; 7 dc ♕xc7 8 ♕d1 ♗b4+ 9 ♗d2 0-0-0 with a strong attack.

7	...	♗xd7

Black has a big lead in development. Staker gives 8 a3 (with the idea of preventing ... ♗b4+ or ... ♘b4) as good for White, but this is a completely wrong assessment, e.g. 8 ... ♕f6 9 ♘c3 (9 ♕g5 ♕xg5 10 ♘xg5 ♘d4 wins) 9 ... ♗e6 and now:

a) **10 ♕e4** ♗c5 11 e3 0-0-0 followed by ... ♖he8 wins.

b) **10 ♕g5** ♕xg5 11 ♘xg5 ♘d4 wins.

c) **10 ♕d1** ♗xc4 11 ♗g5 ♕e6 with advantage to Black.

d) **10 ♕d3** ♘ce5 11 ♕e4 (11 ♘xe5?? ♕xf2+; 11 ♕c2 ♗xc4) 11 ... ♗c5 12 e3 0-0-0 with excellent compensation for the pawn.

In the 4 ♕d5 variation, too, Black gets a good game by attacking the exposed white queen.

B

There are four other moves that occur in practice:

B1 4 e3
B2 4 ♘c3
B3 4 a3
B4 4 e6

B1

4	e3	♘xe5

5 ♘f3 ♘bc6 transposes to Chapter 1.

B2

4	♘c3	♘xe5

5 e3 followed by 6 ♘f3 transposes to Chapter 1 or 5 ♗f4 to Chapter 2.

B3

4	a3	♘xe5

5 b3 g6 6 ♗b2 ♗g7 7 ♕c2 (otherwise ... ♘d3+ and ... ♗xb2) 7 ... 0-0 8 ♘c3 (8 e3 d5! threatening ... ♗f5) 8 ... ♘bc6 9 e3 d6 10 ♗e2 ♖e8 with an active position for Black: 11 ♘f3 ♗f5! 12 e4 ♘xf3+ 13 ♗xf3 ♘d4 14 ♕d1 ♘xf3+ 15 gf (15 ♕xf3? ♗xe4) 15 ... ♕g5 etc.

B4

4	e6

This deserves closer examination. According to *ECO* Black

equalises after 4 ... de 5 ♕xd8+
♔xd8 6 ♘c3 ♗c5 7 e3 ♗d7 8 ♗e2
♘f6 9 ♘f3 ♘c6 10 0-0 a6 11 a3 a5
12 b3 ♔e7 =.

This judgement is not in doubt
but the resulting position is
possibly not to the taste of
adherents of the Budapest Gambit.
Those who are dissatisfied will
find an interesting suggestion in
the following game.

Game 22
Rasin-Ivanov
USSR 1979

(1 d4 ♘f6 2 c4 e5 3 de ♘g4)

4	e6	♗b4+
5	♗d2	♕f6!?
6	ef+	♔xf7
7	♘f3	

White cannot capture the bishop
on b4: 7 ♗xb4? ♕xf2+ 8 ♔d2 ♘e3
followed by ... ♘xf1+.

7	...	♕xb2
8	♗xb4	♕xb4+
9	♘d2	♖e8
10	e3	♕e7
11	h3 (74)	

Black has reached a good
position and should now continue
11 ... ♘f6, e.g. 12 ♗d3 d6 13 0-0
♘bd7 14 ♘b3 (aimed against ...
♘c5) 14 ... a5 15 a4 b6 followed by
... ♗b7, ... ♔g8 etc. Black stands a
little better.

74
B

In the game he continued badly:

11	...	♘e5?
12	♘xe5+	♕xe5
13	♗d3	

As Black no longer has the
important defender, the knight on
f6, White has some chances on the
kingside. Black's further play also
leaves something to be desired.

13	...	g6
14	0-0	♘c6
15	♔h1	♔g7
16	♖b1	♘e7
17	♖b5	d5
18	cd	♘xd5
19	f4	♕d6
20	♘e4	♕d8
21	♕a1+	♘f6
22	♖d1	♖f8
23	g4	♗d7
24	♖d5	♔g8
25	♘xf6+	♖xf6
26	♖xd7	

1-0

5 Fajarowicz Gambit Introduction

1	d4	♘f6
2	c4	e5
3	de	♘e4!? *(75)*

75
W

The idea of this gambit is said to have arisen in Leipzig chess circles. Its international première took place in a tournament in Wiesbaden 1928, in a game between H.Steiner and Fajarowicz. As we will see in Chapter 7, White fell into an almost lost position after only a few moves. This was the birth of a new opening system.

Before we turn to a systematic examination, we consider the starting position of the Fajarowicz Gambit and make a few general observations.

All the white and black pieces are still in their 'starting-blocks' except the black knight. Does the horse stand well or badly? The evaluation of the whole variation depends on the answer to this question.

When in general does a piece stand well? According to generally recognised principles of chess strategy, a piece stands well if it
a) controls many (important) squares.
b) is not easily threatened or driven away.

How does the black knight stand now?

Condition a) is clearly fulfilled. The central square e4 is probably a dream square for the black knight which among other things impedes the natural development ♘b1-c3. Also the point f2 is threatened in some variations.

As far as condition b) is concerned, the case is not so easy to answer. As we will see shortly, the knight on e4 is indeed easy to attack, but resists like an obstinate donkey kicking out wildly! The radical ejection of the knight by **4 f3??** ends in material loss for White after 4 ... ♕h4+ 5 g3 ♘xg3. The black knight indeed dies, but has sold its soul dearly!

It is possible that your opponent will not be at all familiar with the Fajarowicz Gambit and will not absolutely apply the correct strategical considerations. Perhaps his train of thought will run: "I would like to attack the knight on e4 with my f-pawn but this is not possible at once because of ♕h4+. Therefore I'll simply protect the square g3 first and then play f3." This could result in the following variation:

4 ♗f4?! ♘c6 5 f3? (indeed 5 ... ♕h4+ now loses a piece to 6 g3 but ...) 5 ... ♗b4+ 6 ♘d2 ♗xd2+ 7 ♗xd2 ♕h4+ and Black wins. Notice the diversion ... ♗b4+ which is typical of the Fajarowicz Gambit.

The decisive mistake was 5 f3?; after 5 ♘f3 the game transposes into variations with 4 ♘f3 – see

Chapter 8. There all the other untheoretical continuations will be reviewed.

So White can only attack the knight on e4 with pieces. To this end there are only two pieces available at the moment: the knight on b1 and the queen on d1.

The white knight can in theory be developed on c3, but after **4 ♘c3?** ♗b4 Black immediately has the better of it: 5 ♗d2 ♗xc3 6 bc ♘c6 7 ♘f3 ♕e7 or 5 ♕c2 ♘xc3 6 bc ♗a5 7 ♘f3 0-0 8 ♗g5 ♕e8 followed by ... ♘c6 in both cases regaining the pawn with the better game on account of the weak doubled pawns c3/c4.

There remain the following possibilities for White to attack the knight on e4:
Chapter 6:
Various queen moves on the d-file (4 ♕d3; 4 ♕d4; and 4 ♕d5).
Chapter 7:
The attack by 4 ♕c2
Chapter 8:
The system with 4 ♘f3, as well as less common systems.

6 Fajarowicz
4 ♛-moves on the d-file

1	d4	♘f6
2	c4	e5
3	de	♘e4

White can attack the knight on e4 with various queen moves on the d-file.

A   4 ♛d3
B   4 ♛d4
C   4 ♛d5

A

    4   ♛d3 *(76)*

    4   ...   ♘c5

Where should White move the queen?

a) **5 ♛d5?** ♘c6 and White has lost

a tempo in comparison with C (4 ♛d5).

b) **5 ♛c2?** loses a tempo (why not immediately 4 ♛c2 as in Chapter 7?). Demonstration Game 1 illustrates how Black can exploit his opponent's hesitation.

c) **5 ♛c3** transposes to a position which will be reviewed in B. It makes no difference if this position is reached by ♛d4-c3 or ♛d3-c3.

4 ♛d3 only has significance if the white queen can occupy an active post after 4 ... ♘c5. 5 ♛g3 represents such an attempt and will be examined more closely in Demonstration Game 2.

Demonstration Game 1

(1 d4 ♘f6 2 c4 e5 3 de ♘e4)

4	♛d3	♘c5
5	♛c2?	♘c6
6	♘f3	d6
7	♗g5	♛d7! *(77)*

This motif often occurs in the Fajarowicz Gambit. Black avoids the bishop exchange and brings

77
W

his queen to f5 where it can control important squares such as d3 and h5.

8	ed	♗xd6
9	e3	♘b4
10	♕c3	♕f5!

This tactic is also standard: 11 ♕xb4?? naturally fails to ... ♘d3+ and ... ♗xb4+. Furthermore, Black gets the upper hand after 11 ♕xg7 ♘c2+ 12 ♔d1 ♖f8, e.g. 13 ♘d4 ♘xd4 followed by ... ♘e6 winning a piece or 13 ♘h4 ♕xf2 with a clear advantage.

| 11 | ♘a3 | 0-0 |

Threatening 12 ... ♘e4 winning a piece.

| 12 | ♗h4 | ♖e8 |
| 13 | ♖d1 |

The plausible variation 13 ♗e2 ♘bd3+ 14 ♗xd3 ♘xd3+ 15 ♔e2 ♘f4+ 16 ♔f1 ♘xg2 17 ♔xg2 ♕h3+ 18 ♔g1 ♕xf3 illustrates White's difficulties.

13	...	♕h5
14	♗e2	♗g4
15	♗g3

Otherwise ... ♗xf3 wins the bishop on h4.

15	...	♘e4
16	♕b3	♗xg3
17	fg	♘xg3
18	♖g1	♘xe2
19	♔xe2	♗xf3+
20	gf	♕xh2+
21	♔f1	♖ad8
		0-1

White has no satisfactory defence to the numerous threats: 22 ♖xd8 ♖xd8 followed by ... ♖d2 or (after 23 ♘b1) ... ♘d3; 22 ♖g2 ♕h1+; 22 ♖e1 ♖d2; 22 ♘b1 ♘c2 etc.

Demonstration game 2

(1 d4 ♘f6 2 c4 e5 3 de ♘e4)

| 4 | ♕d3?! | ♘c5 |
| 5 | ♕g3 |

Protects the pawn on e5 and impedes the development of the bishop on f8 as the pawn on g7 hangs.

5	...	♘e6
6	♘f3	♘c6
7	e3 *(78)*

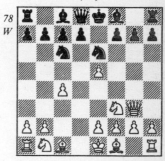

78
W

Apart from the text White has

two other possibilities:

a) 7 ♘c3 ♘b4 and because of the threat 8 ... ♘c2+ White loses the right to castle and his king remains in the centre, which can hardly be good.

b) **7 a3** prevents the sortie 7 ... ♘b4 but does nothing for development. 7 ... d6 (here, and in similar positions, accepting the pawn is fatal) 8 ed? ♗xd6 9 ♕g4 (even worse is 9 ♕h3 ♘ed4 10 ♕h4 ♘c2+; now 9 ... ♘ed4 is met by 10 ♕e4+) 9 ... 0-0 10 ♕e4 (what else against 10 ... ♘ed4) 10 ... ♖e8 11 ♕c2 ♘ed4 12 ♘xd4 ♘xd4 13 ♕d1 ♗f5 and Black wins.

So White may not play 8 ed but after 8 ♘c3 de 9 ♘xe5 ♘xe5 10 ♕xe5 ♗d6 he is again hunted.

7	...	d6
8	♗e2	de
9	♘xe5?!	

Please don't forget that the task of a demonstration game is to answer the constant question "What happens if ..." in most practical cases. Naturally White must not take the pawn on e5 but then Black stands better without material disadvantage.

9	...	♘b4!
10	♘a3	♗d6!

Threatening 11 ... f6. Therefore:

11	f4	♗xe5
12	fe	♘d3+
13	♗xd3	♕xd3
14	♕f2	0-0

15	♕e2	♘c5
16	♕xd3	

16 b4? ♕c3+ etc.

16	...	♘xd3+
17	♔e2	♘xe5
18	h3	

Or Black continues actively with ... ♗g4+.

18	...	♗f5
19	♖d1	♖ad8
20	♖xd8	♖xd8
21	b3	♗e4
22	g3	♗f3+
23	♔f2	♖d1

Prevents 24 ♗b2 because of ... ♖d2+.

24	♘c2	

24 ♘b5 also doesn't help: 24 ... ♗h5 (threatening ... ♘d3+) 25 g4 ♗g6 26 ♔e2 ♖h1 27 ♘xc7 ♘d3 winning a piece.

24	...	♗e4
25	♘e1	

25 ♘d4? ♘d3+ and ... ♖xc1. Now White hopes to free himself with 26 ♔e2.

25	...	♗d3! (79)

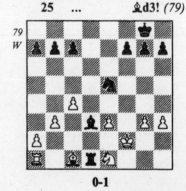

0-1

White is in zugzwang. His rook cannot move, nor his bishop (26 ♗b2 still fails to ... ♖d2+). His knight also has no moves: 26 ♘f3 ♖f1+ and ... ♘xf3; 26 ♘g2 ♖f1 mate. Black can sadistically make tempo moves with his king until White runs out of pawn moves.

Summary

After 4 ♕d3 Black wins a tempo (4 ... ♘c5) and assumes the initiative. After 5 ♕g3 Black secures the point g7 by 5 ... ♘e6 and then advances in the centre (... d6).

B

4   ♕d4

It is clear that the white queen must soon move again as ... ♘c6 is in the air. But first the knight must move and again c5 is right.

4   ...   ♘c5
5   ♘f3   ♘c6 *(80)*

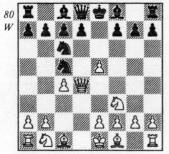

The white queen now has a number of retreats:
a) **6 ♕c3** (already mentioned in A) 6 ... ♘e6 7 a3 (otherwise 7 ... ♗b4)

7 ... g5 8 h3 ♗g7 9 e3 d6 and Black regains the pawn with active play.
b) **6 ♕d5** d6 7 ♗g5 ♕d7 8 ed ♗xd6 9 ♘c3 ♘b4 10 ♕d2 ♘e6 (threatening ... ♘bd3+ to be followed by ... ♘xf2+) 11 e3 ♕g6 *(81)*.

Black has a clear advantage. 12 ... ♘c2+ is threatened and if 12 ♖c1 ♘bd3+ etc.

All other queen moves either lose time (6 ♕d1), obstruct his own pieces (6 ♕d2), or expose the queen to further attack (6 ♕g4 d6; 6 ♕h4 ♗e7; 6 ♕f4 ♘e6).

Thus 4 ♕d4 is unsatisfactory.

C

4   ♕d5 *(82)*

4 ...　　　　♗b4+!

Others that have occurred in practice:

a) **4 ... ♘c5?** (bad here!) 5 ♘f3 ♘c6 6 ♗g5 ♗e7 7 ♕xc5! ♗xg5 8 ♘c3 b6 9 ♕d5 ♗b7 10 e6! (double attack on the bishop on g5) 10 ... f6 11 ♘xg5 fg 12 ♕xd7+ ♕xd7 13 ed+ ♔xd7 14 0-0-0+ and White won, Olsen-Martinsen, corres 1945.

An important hint: after 4 ♕d3 and 4 ♕d4, 4 ... ♘c5 is the best move. After 4 ♕d5, on the other hand, it is wrong! There are only a few variations where you can go seriously astray – it's in your own interest to make the effort to remember them!

b) **4 ... f5** 5 ef ♘xf6 6 ♕e5+? ♗e7 7 ♗g5 ♘c6 8 ♕e3 0-0 9 ♘c3? ♗g4 10 ♗xe7 ♘xe7 11 ♕g3 ♘xf2 0-1, Camara-Flores, Sao Paolo 1937. Camara didn't have his best day.

After 4 ... f5 theoreticians regard 5 ♘d2 c6 6 ♕d3 d5 7 ed ♕a5 8 a3 ♗xd6 as equal.

After 4 ... ♗b4+ White now has:

C1 5 ♗d2

C2 5 ♘d2

C1

5	♗d2	♘xd2
6	♘xd2	♘c6
7	♘gf3	♕e7
8	0-0-0	♗xd2+
9	♖xd2	

After 9 ♕xd2 or 9 ♘xd2 Black

equalises comfortably with 9 ... ♘xe5.

The column game is Blumich-Fajarowicz, match 1930. Black could now have had a good game with 9 ... ♘b4 winning the pawn on a2 or, after 10 ♕a5 b6 11 ♕a4 ♘c6, with good play against the pawn on e5; the white queen stands a little offside.

C2

5	♘d2	♘c5
6	a3	

Or 6 ♘gf3 0-0 7 g3 b6! and if 8 ♕xa8 then 8 ... ♗b7 9 ♕xa7 ♘c6 winning the queen.

6	...	b6!! (83)
7	♗xd2	

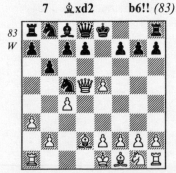

Another standard combination in the Fajarowicz Gambit (suggested by J.Staker). The idea is to trap the queen after 8 ♕xa8 ♗b7 9 ♕xa7 ♘c6. Notice that this combination is only made possible by the move a3, which takes a retreat square from the white queen. Therefore Black delays ... b6 until a3 is played.

In the diagram Black threatens a knight fork with 8 ... ♗b7 9 ♛d4 ♘b3.

8	♛f3	♗b7
9	♛g3	0-0
10	♗h6	

Or 10 ♘f3 ♘e4 11 ♛f4 ♘xd2 12 ♛xd2 ♘c6 13 e3 ♖e8 14 ♛c3 ♛e7 followed by 15 ... ♘xe5 and Black stands well (the bishop on b7 is more active than its opposite number).

10	...	♘e6
11	♘f3	♘c6
12	♗d2	

After 12 e3 f6 the bishop on h6 gets into difficulties (... ♔h8).

12	...	♘cd4
13	♘xd4	♘xd4

14	♛d3	♘c6
15	♗c3	♛e7

Black stands well. He regains the pawn with ... ♘xe5 and has well-placed pieces (bishop on b7, knight on e5). The attempt to maintain the extra pawn by 16 f4 or 16 ♛d5 looks very risky, as Black then plays 16 ... ♖ad8 and follows with ... d6 gaining a strong initiative.

Summary

Excursions of the white queen along the d-file bring nothing for White. On d3 it is molested by ... ♘c5, on d4 by ... ♘c6. d5 is also no place for the lady, for the black bishop soon appears on b7 with an unmistakeable invitation to move.

7 Fajarowicz 4 ♕c2

1	d4	♘f6
2	c4	e5
3	de	♘e4
4	♕c2	(84)

84
B

In Chapter 6 we saw various queen moves on the d-file. Black was able to attack the exposed queen with one of his knights and thus gain a lead in development and the better game. 4 ♕c2 also attacks the 'Fajarowicz knight' but this time from a safer distance. It is 4 ♕c2 that gives Black the most problems to solve.

The material is divided up as follows:

A 4 ... d5 5 *various*
B 4 ... d5 5 ed ♗f5 6 *not* ♘c3
C 4 ... d5 5 ed ♗f5 6 ♘c3
D 4 ... ♗b4+

A

| 4 | ... | d5 (85) |

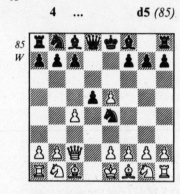

85
W

5 ♘f3?

This tame move was played in Game 23. The correct 5 ed will be examined in the next sections. Other possibilities are:

a) **5 e3?!** ♘c6 6 ♘f3 ♗f5 7 ♕d1 dc 8 ♕xd8+ ♖xd8 9 ♗xc4 ♗b4+ 10 ♔e2 ♘a5 with advantage to Black in Rubinstein-Becker, Vienna 1932 (11 ♗d3? ♖xd3 12 ♔xd3 ♘xf2+ etc; 11 ♗b3 ♘xb3 12 ab ♘c5 followed by ... ♗d3+; 11 ♗b5+ c6 12 ♗a4 ♘c5 followed by ... ♗d3+).

b) **5 cd** ♕xd5 6 ♘d2 ♗b4 7 ♘gf3 ♘c6 8 a3 ♗xd2+ 9 ♗xd2 (9 ♘xd2? ♗f5) 9 ... ♘xd2 10 ♕xd2 ♕xd2+ 11 ♘xd2 (or 11 ♔xd2 ♗g4 followed

by ... 0-0-0 and ... ♖he8) 11 ...
♘xe5 with equality. Black's best
set-up is ... ♗e6, ... 0-0-0 and ...
♖he8.

Game 23
Mititelu-Seineanu
Romania 1955

(1 d4 ♘f6 2 c4 e5 3 de ♘e4 4 ♕c2 d5)

　5　♘f3?　　♗f5

As we will see in B, the bishop
on f5 and the queen on c2 are
natural enemies. On account of
the threat ... ♘g3 the stronger one
must move away.

　6　♕a4+　　♘c6
　7　♗e3

The natural 7 e3 leads to a very
good game for Black after 7 ...
♘c5 8 ♕d1 (else the white queen is
lost: 8 ♕b5?? a6; 8 ♕a3?? ♘d3+!)
8 ... ♘b4 9 ♘a3 c6! followed by 10
... ♕a5 and/or ... ♘bd3. Therefore
White decides to control the square
c5, but also without any luck.

　7　...　　♗b4+
　8　♘bd2　　d4!
　9　♗f4

Naturally 9 ♘xd4 fails to 9 ...
♗xd2+.

　9　...　　g5
　10　a3

If 10 ♗g3 g4 and one of the
knights is lost.

　10　...　　♘c5!
　11　♕d1　　gf
　12　ab　　♘xb4
　13　♖c1　　d3! *(86)*

White's position is a picture of
misery. Unfortunately the rest of
this game is not extant. It is only
known that Black won. White will
lose at least the exchange with a
miserable position.

Summary

The sortie ... ♗f5 which threatens
the white queen or creates discovered threats must be taken
seriously. White has no time for
slack moves. The knight on e4 must
be deprived of protection.

B

　5　ed　　♗f5 *(87)*

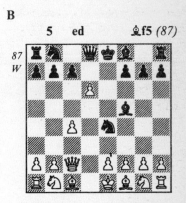

The games in the following

three sections illustrate the commonly played moves. 6 ♘c3! is in C.

B1 6 dc?

B2 6 ♕a4+?

B3 6 ♕b3?

B1

6   dc?

Game 24
Rössner-Kipke
Berlin 1933

(1 d4 ♘f6 2 c4 e5 3 de ♘e4 4 ♕c2 d5 5 ed ♗f5)

6   dc?

White's overlarge appetite will not do him any good.

6	...	♕xc7
7	♕b3	♘c6
8	♘f3	0-0-0
9	e3	♘c5

White is already lost. If 10 ♕c3 there follows 10 ... ♘b4 11 ♘a3 ♘e4 12 ♕b3 ♕a5 13 ♔e2 (13 ♗d2 ♘xd2 14 ♘xd2 ♘c2+) 13 ... ♘c5 14 ♕c3 ♗d3+ with deadly discoveries. So he makes a last try:

10   ♕a3!? (88)

88
B

Normally ♕a3 would be bad on account of the standard combination ... ♘d3+ and ... ♗xa3. Here, by way of exception, this combination is inadequate: 10 ... ♘d3+ 11 ♗xd3 ♗xa3 12 ♗xf5+ ♔b8 13 ♘xa3 and White would have 'half the board' for the queen.

However, Black can realise his advantage in a different way.

10   ...   ♘b4!

Now naturally 11 ♕xb4?? ♘d3+ 12 ♗xd3 ♗xb4+ would be completely hopeless. 11 ♘d4 ♖xd4 and 12 ... ♘c2+ is also won for Black.

11   ♕xa7   ♘c2+
0-1

There could follow 12 ♔e2 ♗d3+ 13 ♔d1 (13 ♔d2 ♘e4+) 13 ... ♘xa1 etc.

Another horrible example on the same theme:

Game 25
Krastev-Donev
Bulgaria 1954

(1 d4 ♘f6 2 c4 e5 3 de ♘e4 4 ♕c2 d5 5 ed ♗f5)

6	dc?	♕xc7
7	♕a4+	♘c6
8	♘f3	0-0-0

Again threatening ... ♘c5 and ... ♘b4. White now wants to protect b4 . . .

9	♗d2	♕b6

. . . but comes up against two nasty threats: ... ♕xb2 winning a rook and ... ♕xf2+. He chose:

10	♕b3	♕xf2+
11	♔d1	♗b4
12	♔c1	

Or 12 ♘c3 ♗xc3 13 bc ♖xd2+!
14 ♘xd2 ♖d8 etc.

12	...	♘xd2
13	♘bxd2	♖xd2!
14	♘xd2	♕e1+
15	♕d1	♗xd2 mate

A rare and pretty mate.

Summary

6 dc? increases Black's already
dangerous initiative. Furthermore,
it opens the d-file, but only for the
entry of the black rook! So: hands
off the pawn on c7!

B2

| 6 | ♕a4+ |

Game 26
H.Steiner-Fajarowicz
Wiesbaden 1928

(1 d4 ♘f6 2 c4 e5 3 de ♘e4 4 ♕c2
d5 5 ed ♗f5)

| 6 | ♕a4+ *(89)* |

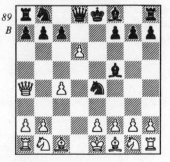

White's queen voluntarily leaves
the line of fire of the bishop on f5.

| 6 | ... | ♘c6 |
| 7 | ♘f3 | |

7 dc leads to positions similar to
those in games 2 and 3.

| 7 | ... | ♗xd6 |
| 8 | a3 | |

Directed against ... ♘c5 followed
by ... ♘b4 threatening c2.

| 8 | ... | ♕f6 |
| 9 | g3 | |

White does not want to weaken
the square d3 (for which, as we
have just seen, the black knight
sometimes aims) and prepares to
build a safe haven for his king (g3,
♗g2, 0-0). However, he does not
manage to castle.

| 9 | ... | 0-0-0 |
| 10 | ♘bd2 | |

If immediately 10 ♗g2, then 10
... ♘c5 11 ♕d1 ♗xg3. Therefore
White closes the d-file.

10	...	♘c5
11	♕d1	♖he8
12	♗g2	♗d3!
13	e3	♗e5
14	♘xe5	

It is easy to say that White
should have done something else,
but what?

| 14 | ... | ♘xe5 |
| 15 | f4 | ♗xc4! *(90)* |

As far as the opening is concerned, the world première of the
Fajarowicz Gambit has completely
succeeded. Black has a winning

90
W

position. 16 fe?? is out of the
question because of 16 ... ♘d3+
and 17 ... ♕f2 mate and after 16
♗f1 ♘ed3+ 17 ♗xd3 ♘xd3+ 18
♔e2 or 18 ♔f1 White loses his
queen to 18 ... ♘xb2+.

And so, 0-1? – Not at all!

16   ♔f2

Here Black could have driven
home the coffin nail immediately:
16 ... ♘ed3+ 17 ♔g1 (or 17 ♔f3
♕c6+ 18 e4 ♖xe4 etc) 17 ... ♖xe3
18 ♘f3 ♖e1+! (19 ♘xe1 ♕d4+
and mates; 19 ♕xe1 ♘xe1 etc).

16	...	♗e6?
17	h3!	♘b3
18	♔g1	♘xa1
19	fe	♕xe5
20	♕f3	♗d5
21	e4	♗c6
22	♔h2	♘c2
23	♕xf7	♖f8?!

Simpler was 23 ... ♘e3 followed
by 24 ... ♘xg2 or, if 24 ♗f3, 24 ...
♖xd2! 25 ♗xd2 ♕xb2 etc.

24	♕b3	♘d4
25	♕c3	♖f2

26	♖e1	♖df8
27	♔h1	♕f6
28	♖f1	♖xf1+
29	♘xf1	*(91)*

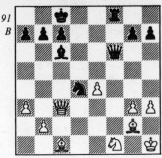

91
B

Black is still winning, for example
after 29 ... ♗xe4!, but now, un-
believably, he played:

29   ...   ♕xf1+??

Did Fajarowicz see some sort of
mating net? Unfortunately we can
no longer ask him.

30	♗xf1	♖xf1+
31	♔g2	

1-0?

Black was probably completely
unnerved by his blunder for he
could still fight on with 31 ... ♘e2
32 ♕e3 ♖xc1 33 ♕xe2 b5! (with
the idea ... ♖c4, followed by ...
♔b7) and White is still far from
winning.

The curious end to this game
does not alter the fact that the variation in this section is advantageous
for Black. The white queen finds
no peace on a4 as it is chased by ...
♘c5. The same applies to the next
game, where she moves to b3.

B3

6 ♕b3

Game 27
Gilfer-Richter
Munich Ol 1936

(1 d4 ♘f6 2 c4 e5 3 de ♘e4 4 ♕c2 d5 5 ed ♗f5)

6 ♕b3 ♗xd6
7 ♘d2

7 ♕xb7? 0-0 8 ♕xa8?? ends in disaster: 8 ... ♗b4+ 9 ♗d2 ♗xd2+ 10 ♔d1 ♘xf2 mate.

7 ... 0-0
8 ♕xb7?

Relatively better was 8 ♘gf3 though Black still has a very active game after 8 ... ♘c5 9 ♕c3 ♘c6 10 a3 a5 11 e3 ♖e8 12 ♗e2 ♗e7! followed by ... ♗f6 or 9 ♕d1 ♘c6 10 a3 a5 11 e3 ♘d3+. Now, however, White's ship goes under very quickly.

8 ... ♗c5!
9 e3

Forced. The knight on e4 is naturally taboo: 9 ♘xe4 ♗xe4 10 ♕xe4?? ♗b4+ and mates. 9 ♕xa8 ♗xf2+ 10 ♔d1 ♗e3 11 ♘gf3 ♘f2+ 12 ♔e1 ♗e4 results in a very original trapping of the queen.

9 ... ♕e7! *(92)*

Eying the point e3, e.g.

a) 10 ♕xa8 ♘xd2 (threatening ... ♗e4) 11 f3 ♕xe3+ etc.

b) 10 ♘gf3 ♘xf2! 11 ♗xf2 ♕xe3+ 12 ♔g3 ♗d6+ 13 ♔h4 ♕h6 mate.

Therefore the contorted text

move – the point e3 must be protected. White's position is still beyond salvation. He definitely overstepped the mark with 7 ♕xb7. The rest is easily comprehensible.

10 ♘df3 ♗b4+
11 ♗d2 ♘xd2
12 ♘xd2 ♗e4

13 ♕b5 ♖d8 14 0-0-0 ♕d6 15 ♘gf3 ♗xf3 16 gf ♗xd2+ 17 ♔b1 ♘c6 18 c5 ♕g6+ 19 e4 ♖ab8 20 ♕c4 ♕f6 21 b3 ♘a5 0-1.

If 22 ♕c2 ♕xf3 23 ♖g1 ♘xb3 etc.

Summary

If the white queen moves from c2, it goes out of the frying pan into the fire. The "Fajarowicz knight" on e4 finds a fine square on c5 with gain of tempo.

Is the source of the trouble to be found in 4 ♕c2? As we will see in C, this is not the case. Only the moves 6 ♕b3 and ♕a4 are bad. White has a much stronger continuation at his sixth move.

C

4	...	d5
5	ed	♗f5
6	♘c3! (93)	

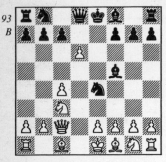

In this way the strength of the knight discovery is considerably reduced. With ♘c3 White once again covers the square e4 so that moves of the black knight can be answered by e4. The following illustrative game acquaints us with the refinements of this variation.

Game 28
Kottnauer-Martin
Czechoslovakia v. France 1946

(1 d4 ♘f6 2 c4 e5 3 de ♘e4 4 ♕c2 d5 5 ed ♗f5)

| 6 | ♘c3! | ♘xd6 |

Black has no other moves:
a) **6 ... ♘g3 7 ♕a4+ ♗d7 8 dc ♕xc7 9 ♘b5!**.
b) **6 ... ♘xf2? 7 ♕xf5 ♘xh1 8 ♗g5**
c) **6 ... ♘xc3 7 ♕xf5 ♘a4 8 ♕b5+ ♕d7 9 ♕xb7** with a winning position for White in all cases.

| 7 | e4! | ♘xe4 (94) |

Black has scarcely any choice: 7 ... ♕e7 8 ♗d3 ♘c6 9 ♘ge2 ♗g6 (9 ... ♘b4?? 10 ♕a4+) 10 ♘d5 with a clear advantage to White.

Before we look at the actual course of the game, we must without fail become familiar with the important alternative **8 ♘xe4**. In this variation Black must play for a long time with a piece less. Admittedly, he has a powerful initiative for it. In short, it is playing with fire – for both players. However, players of the Fajarowicz Gambit may not avoid risks.

Acceptance of the piece sacrifice – **8 ... ♗b4+ 9 ♔e2** (9 ♗d2 ♗xd2+ 10 ♕xd2 ♗xe4 11 ♕xd8+ ♔xd8 12 0-0-0+ ♔c8 with equality) **9 ... ♘c6 10 ♗e3 ♕e7 11 f3 0-0-0** (95) – is, according to analysis by IM Nikola Minev in *ECO*, better for Black. Up to now nobody has shown the desire to doubt this opinion and play the position with the white pieces, so we must forgo practical examples.

95
W

Some possibilities:

a) **12 a3** ♖d2+ **13** ♗xd2 ♘d4+ **14** ♔f2 ♘xc2 **15** ♗xb4 ♘xb4 **16** ab ♛xb4 is good for Black as White's kingside is still undeveloped.

b) **12** ♘d6+ ♖xd6 **13** ♛xf5+ ♖e6! **14** ♔f2 g6 **15** ♛h3 (15 ♛d3 ♖xe3 followed by ... ♗c5) **15** ... f5 **16** ♗f4 ♖e1 wins (17 ♖xe1 ♛xe1 mate; 17 ♗c1 ♖xf1+! 18 ♔xf1?? ♛e1 mate).

c) **12** ♔f2 ♖he8 and now:

c1) **13** ♘d6+ ♖xd6 **14** ♛xf5+ ♔b8 **15** ♛f4 (15 ♗f4 ♖e1+!! 16 ♖xe1 ♗xe1 mate) **15** ... ♖f6 **16** ♛g5 h6 and wins as e3 can no longer be defended.

c2) **13** ♗d3 ♗g6 (threatening ... f5) **14** g4 (White can hardly be enthusiastic about 14 a3 f5 15 ab ♘xb4 16 ♛a4 ♘xd3+ 17 ♔f1 fe 18 ♛xa7 ef) **14** ... ♘e5 **15** ♖d1 ♛h4+ **16** ♔g2 ♘xg4 **17** fg ♛xg4+ **18** ♔f2 (18 ♘g3 ♖xe3) **18** ... ♗xe4 **19** ♗xe4 ♛xd1 with advantage to Black.

An exhaustive analysis is not feasible for the number of possible variations is very great. Black's conduct of the attack is associated in many cases with ... ♖e8, ... ♗g6 and ... f5.

Experience shows that in a practical game the attacker has better chances than the defender. For one thing the art of defence is significantly more difficult to learn than that of attack, for another mistakes are much more likely to be committed by the defender; he must pay heed to a whole host of threats while the attacker (after making his selection from the possible variations) can concentrate on only one continuation. Also such factors as use of energy, use of time and nervousness come into play and in all cases the defender is at a disadvantage.

This explains the large number of attacking victories which proved to be not completely correct in analysis, but which succeeded at the board.

In short, given a ration of courage and good tactical ability, the variation given above offers Black good practical prospects – a verdict with which *ECO* agrees.

After this long diversion we return to our illustrative game (see diagram 94), in which Kottnauer chose a continuation which was significantly more unpleasant for

Black:

8	♗d3!	♘xf2
9	♗xf5	♘xh1
10	♘f3 (96)	

This position is of decisive importance for the fate of the variation 4 ♕c2 d5. Before we devote ourselves to its analysis, we will look at the course of our illustrative game:

10	...	♗c5?
11	♘e4	♕e7
12	♗g5	f6

12 ... ♗b4+ 13 ♔e2 f6 14 ♗e3 wins – Reuben Fine.

13   0-0-0

An ingenious piece sacrifice that Black can hardly accept: 13 ... fg 14 ♘xc5 ♕xc5 15 ♕e4+ ♕e7 16 ♕xb7 0-0 17 ♕xa8 ♘f2 18 ♕d5+ ♔h8 19 ♖e1 with great advantage to White.

13	...	♘a6
14	♖d7 (97)	

The board is in flames! White is temporarily the exchange and a pawn down and his bishop on g5 is

hanging, but his entire army is ideally placed for attack. Moreover, the knight on h1 is trapped.

In the game Black sacrifices his queen. The alternative is 14 ... ♕f8 15 ♕e2! ♗e7 16 ♘e5!! and now:

a) **16 ... fg** 17 ♕h5+ g6 18 ♗xg6+ hg 19 ♕xg6+ ♕f7 20 ♕xf7 mate.

b) **16 ... g6** 17 ♘xf6+ ♗xf6 18 ♘xg6+ etc.

c) **16 ... fe** 17 ♖xe7+ ♕xe7 18 ♗xe7 ♔xe7 19 ♕e1! ♖hf8 20 ♗h3 and 21 ♕xh1.

Thus 14 ... ♕f8 would also not save Black. The rest is understandable without much comment.

14	...	♕xd7
15	♗xd7+	♔xd7
16	♘xc5+	♘xc5
17	♕f5+	♘e6
18	♘d4	♖ae8
19	♕d5+	♔c8
20	♘xe6	fg
21	♘c5	♖e1+

After 21 ... ♖hf8 Black gets mated: 22 ♕xb7+ ♔d8 23 ♕d5+ ♔e7 (23 ... ♔c8 24 ♕a8 mate) 24

♕e6+ ♔d8 25 ♕d7 mate.

22	♔d2	♖he8
23	♕xb7+	♔d8
24	♕b8+	♔e7
25	♕xe8+	1-0

If 25 ... ♔xe8 26 ♔xe1 followed by ♔f1-g1xh1 etc.

An impressive victory by White! Nevertheless, we don't want to forget that Black blundered on his 10th move, so we return to the critical position . . .
(1 d4 ♘d6 2 c4 e5 3 de ♘e4 4 ♕c2 d5 5 ed ♗f5 6 ♘c3 ♘xc6 7 e4 ♘xe4 8 ♗d3 ♘xf2 9 ♗xf5 ♘xh1)

10 ♘f3

. . . and confirm that 10 ... ♗d6? 11 ♘e4 ♗xh2 (with the idea 12 ♘xh2 ♕h4+) 12 ♗g5! gives White the advantage.

We make some deliberations however:

If White wants to castle he must play ♗d2 and 0-0-0. Then the knight on h1 can escape via f2.

Naturally White can play ♗e3 and ♔e2 followed by ♖xh1. In this case the knight on h1 is not saved, but at what price; the white king will hardly find peace in the middle of the board. Black will therefore quickly put his heavy pieces on the e-file.

White has two minor pieces (after he has won the knight on h1); Black has a rook and a pawn. Accordingly Black must try to take central outposts from the enemy pieces, to which purpose he places his extra pawns (see later 10 ... g6, 11 ... c6, 12 ... f5). The black rooks must occupy the two open central files.

So we construct a demonstration game, not forgetting that the course of this game is in no way forced, but is only meant to illustrate ideas and plans.

Demonstration Game 3

(1 d4 ♘f6 2 c4 e5 3 de ♘e4 4 ♕c2 d5 5 ed ♗f5 6 ♘c3 ♘xd6 7 e4 ♘xe4 8 ♗d3 ♘xf2 9 ♗xf5 ♘xh1 10 ♘f3 g6)

Black begins the plan of reducing outposts in the centre.

11 ♗e4 *(98)*

11 ♗g5? ♗e7 12 ♗xe7 ♕xe7+ 13 ♗e4 f5 wins; 11 ♕e4+? ♗e7 12 ♗h3 0-0 and 13 ... ♖e8; 11 ♗d3 ♘c6 12 a3 ♕e7+ 13 ♕e2 0-0-0 14 ♕xe7 ♗xe7 15 ♔e2 ♖he8 with an attack.

| 11 | ... | c6 |

The important square d5 is made unavailable to the white pieces.

12   ♗e3

Again 12 ♗g5 ♗e7 13 ♗xe7 ♕xe7 plays into Black's hands; he will bring his heavy pieces to the e-file.

12	...	f5
13	♗d3	♕e7
14	♕e2	

14 ♔d2 ♘a6 followed by ... 0-0-0 with an attack on the d-file.

14	...	♘a6
15	0-0-0	0-0-0
16	♖xh1	

16 ♗xa7? ♗h6+ 17 ♔b1 ♕xe2 18 ♘xe2 c5! 19 ♗b6 ♘f2! and wins.

16	...	♘b4
17	♗b1	♗g7
18	♗g5 *(99)*	

18 a3 ♗xc3 19 bc ♘a6 with the threats 20 ... f4 and 20 ... ♕xa3+; if 18 ♕f2 ♘d3+ 19 ♗xd3 ♖xd3 with the attack; or 18 ♖e1 ♖he8 and Black has splendid development.

18   ...   ♕xe2

19	♘xe2	♖de8
20	♘ed4	c5
21	♘b5	♖e2
22	♗d2	

22 ♘c3? ♗xc3 23 bc ♘xa2+.

22	...	♖d8
23	♘xa7+	

23 ♘c3 ♖xg2; or 23 g3 ♖f2.

23	...	♔b8
24	♘b5	♖xg2
25	♗f4+	♔a8
26	♗e5	

Nothing good comes from 26 ♘c7+ ♔a7 27 ♘b5+.

26	...	♗xe5
27	♘xe5	♖dd2
28	a3 *(100)*	

Or 28 h4 ♖xb2 29 h5 ♘xa2+ 30 ♗xa2 ♖xa2 31 ♔b1 ♖gb2+ 32 ♔c1 ♖h2!.

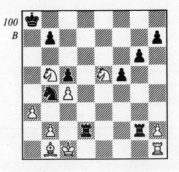

28	...	♘c6
29	♘xc6	bc
30	♘c3	♖xb2
31	h4	♖b3
32	♘d1	h5
33	a4	♖b4
34	♗c2	♖xc4

35	♘e3	♖gxc2+
36	♘xc2	♖xa4
37	♖e1	

37 ♘e3?? ♖a1+; 37 ♖g1 ♖g4!.

37	...	♖xh4
38	♖e6	♖g4
39	♖xc6	h4
40	♘e3	

40 ♖xc5 h3 41 ♖c3 h2 42 ♖h3 ♖g1+ etc.

40	...	h3!
41	♘xg4	fg
42	♖xg6	h2
43	♖h6	g3
44	♔d2	g2

0-1

Summary

This pretty demonstration game should not disguise the fact that there are problems to be solved in the variation with 6 ♘c3. On the other hand Black has many active counterchances in the plan with 10 ... g6.

Only tournament practice can give a definitive answer with regard to the playability of this variation. A player who is familiar with the particularities of this variation can, however, happily employ it in his games.

D

4	...	♗b4+ *(101)*

The four previous sections have shown the many attacking possibilities in the variation 4 ♕c2 d5.

101
W

Those who find the resulting sacrificial dance too hot can put their trust in an idea of the master Hermann Steiner.

After the bishop check 5 ♗d2 is obviously harmless: 5 ... ♘xd2 6 ♘xd2 ♘c6 7 ♘f3 (7 f4? here and in similar positions is not good: 7 ... d6 8 ed ♕xd6 9 e3 0-0 10 ♘f3 ♖e8 11 ♔f2 ♗c5 12 ♖e1 ♕xf4! etc or 8 ♘f3 de followed by 9 ... ♕e7) 7 ... ♕e7 and Black regains his pawn (8 ♕e4 d6!) and has the better game on account of his bishop pair. We therefore consider:

D1 5 ♘d2

D2 5 ♘c3!

D1

5	♘d2	d5

White has three plausible moves:
a) **6 cd** transposes to A of Chapter 7. We saw there that the situation is satisfactory for Black.

b) **6 e3** – see game 29.

c) **6 ed** – see games 30-32.

Game 29
Timet-Meyer
Zagreb 1953

(1 d4 ♘f6 2 c4 e5 3 de ♘e4 4 ♕c2
♗b4+)

5	♘d2	d5
6	e3	♗f5
7	♗d3	♕g5!
8	g3	♘d7
9	♘gf3	♕g4 (102)

With the threat ... ♕xf3!. This
threat would be better executed by
9 ... ♕h5 – see analysis at the end
of the game.

10	0-0	♗xd2
11	♘xd2	♘xd2
12	♗xf5	

Here the black queen is attacked
which it would not be after 9 ...
♕h5.

12	...	♘f3+
13	♔h1	♕h5
14	♗xd7+	♔xd7
15	♔g2	♘h4+
16	gh	♕g4+
17	♔h1	♕f3+

18	♔g1	♕g4+

½-½

From the diagram Black could
play better and obtain a clear
advantage.

9	...	♕h5!
10	0-0	♗xd2
11	♘xd2	♘xe5
12	♗xe4	

12 ♘xe4?? ♘f3+ 13 ♔g2 ♗h3+
14 ♔h1 ♗xf1 and wins.

12	...	de (103)

There is now the deadly threat of
13 ... ♕h3 and 14 ... ♘f3+ or 14 ...
♘g4. 13 ♘xe4 fails to 13 ... ♘f3+
followed by 14 ... ♗h3+ and 15 ...
♗xf1 and after 13 h4 0-0-0 Black
threatens 14 ... ♖xd2! followed by
... ♘f3+ and ... ♕g4 with a mating
attack. 13 ♕a4+ c6 only removes
the queen from the kingside.

13	f4	ef
14	e4	♗h3
15	♖f2	0-0-0
16	♘f1	♘d3

and Black wins. 17 ♖d2?? ♕c5+;
17 ♗e3 ♘xf2 with a decisive ma-

terial advantage.

The passive 6 e3 brought White no luck. In the following illustrative games several players tried 6 ed.

6	ed	♗f5 *(104)*

This is the starting position of the following three interesting, if not mistake-free, games. The theoretical continuation runs:

7	a3	♗xd2+
8	♗xd2	♕xd6

Black has abundant compensation for the sacrificed pawn, e.g. 9 ♕c1 (avoiding the discovery ... ♘g3) 9 ... ♘c6 10 e3 (after 10 ♗f4 ♕e7 11 e3 0-0-0 12 ♘f3 ♘a5 threatening ... ♘b3 Black stands clearly better) 10 ... 0-0-0 11 ♗e2 g5 with a very active game. To be considered is:

9	g4!?	

With the idea 9 ... ♗g6 10 ♗g2! ♘g3 11 ♕a4+ etc.

9	...	♕xd2+

9 ... ♘xd2? 10 ♕xf5 followed by ♕e4+.

10	♕xd2	♘xd2

Chances are level. The game could continue 11 gf ♘xc4 12 ♖c1 ♘d6 13 f6 (13 ♖xc7 ♘c6 14 ♗g2 ♔d8 is good for Black) 13 ... c6 14 fg ♖g8 15 e3 ♘d7 16 ♘e2 0-0-0 17 ♗h3 ♖xg7 18 ♘g3 and the result is still open.

In the following games we will see that White does better to play the above theoretical variation as divergences have not proved good:

Game 30
Antainen-Nieminen
Finnish Corres Ch 1973

(1 d4 ♘f6 2 c4 e5 3 de ♘e4 4 ♕c2 ♗b4+ 5 ♘d2 d5)

6	ed	♗f5
7	dc	♕xc7
8	♕a4+	♘c6
9	♘f3	0-0-0
10	a3	♗xd2+
11	♗xd2	♘xd2
12	♘xd2	♖xd2!
13	♔xd2	♕e5! *(105)*

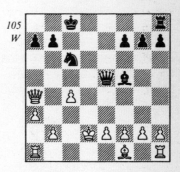

This position had occurred in Müss-Reinhardt, corres 1935. After

14 ♔e1 ♕xb2 15 ♖d1 ♗c2 Black
won without trouble.

Also after **14 ♕b5 ♖d8+ 15 ♔e1**
♘d4! followed by 16 ... ♘c2 (mate)
or 16 ♔c1 ♕f4+ 17 e3 ♕xf2 Black
wins in a few moves.

14	♕b3	♖d8+
15	♔c1	♘a5
16	♕f3	♗e4
17	♕e3(?)	

17 ♕h3+ ♔b8 would have pro-
longed the suffering a little.

| 17 | ... | ♕d6 |

0-1

Mate by 18 ... ♕d1 or 18 b4
♕d1+ 19 ♔b2 ♕c2 can only be
prevented by 18 ♕d3 but after 18
... ♗xd3 one would do better to
save postage on correspondence
cards.

Game 31
Bascau-Meewes
corres 1971

(1 d4 ♘f6 2 c4 e5 3 de ♘e4 4 ♕c2
♗b4+ 5 ♘d2 d5)

6	ed	♗f5
7	♕b3	♘c6
8	dc	

On 8 e3 can follow 8 ... ♕xd6 9
♘f3 0-0-0 10 ♕d1 ♘e5 11 ♘xe5
♘xd2 and wins.

8	...	♕xc7
9	♘f3	0-0-0
10	e3	g5

To drive away the knight on f3,
after which the knight on d2 falls.
11 h3 h5 renews the threat ... g4;

11 a3 ♕a5 already wins the knight
on d2 (12 ♕d1 g4).

11	♘d4	♖xd4!
12	ed	♘xd4
13	♕d1	♕f4!

0-1

An analysis of the above position
is naturally superfluous, but the
mates which arise, even after a
desperate queen sacrifice, are really
not commonplace:

| 14 | f3 | ♕e3+ |
| 15 | ♕e2 | |

Otherwise ... ♕f2 mate.

15	...	♘c2+
16	♔d1	♘f2+
17	♕xf2	♕xf2

18 ♗e2 ♘e3 mate; 18 ♘e4 ♖d8+
19 ♗d2 ♘e3+ 20 ♔c1 ♕e1+! 21
♗xe1 ♖d1 mate. White's position
may well approach a chess player's
nightmare.

Game 32
Laghkva-Contendini
Leipzig Ol 1960

(1 d4 ♘f6 2 c4 e5 3 de ♘e4 4 ♕c2
♗b4+ 5 ♘d2 d5)

6	ed	♗f5
7	♕a4+	♘c6
8	a3	♘c5!
9	dc?	

White also stands very medi-
ocrely after 9 ♕d1 ♘d4 10 e4
♗xd2+ 11 ♗xd2 ♗xe4 but now
follows a short procedure:

| 9 | ... | ♕e7! |

Another standard trap of the

diabolical Mr Fajarowicz!

10 ♕d1 ♘d3 mate

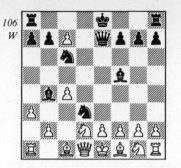

This trap should impress itself on everyone – and be avoided with White if possible!

D2

5 ♘c3 d5
6 ed

6 cd ♕xd5 7 ♗d2 ♗xc3 8 ♗xc3 ♘xc3 9 ♕xc3 ♘c6 10 ♘f3 0-0 11 e3 ♖e8 etc with equality.

6 ... ♗f5 *(107)*

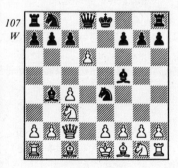

7 ♗d2

a) **7 dc** is, as in previous variations, not adequate: 7 ... ♕xc7 8 ♗d2 ♗xc3 9 ♗xc3 ♘g3! 10 e4 ♗xe4 11 ♗d3 ♗xd3 12 ♕xd3 ♘xh1 13 ♗xg7 ♖g8 14 ♕xh7 ♕e7+ 15 ♘e2 ♖xg7 16 ♕xg7 ♘d7 followed by 17 ... 0-0-0. In this complicated position Black's chances are to be preferred.

b) **7 ♕b3** occurred in Deutgen-Schmid, Celle 1948: 7 ... ♘c6 8 ♘f3 ♗xd6 9 e3 0-0-0 10 ♗e2 ♕g6 11 ♘h4 ♕f6 12 ♘xf5 ♕xf5 13 0-0 (or 13 f3, 13 f4, 13 ♗f3) 13 ... ♘c5! 0-1, because the queen is trapped.

7 ... ♘xd6
8 e4

An important alternative is 8 ♕b3 ♘c6 9 e3 ♕e7 10 ♘f3 (10 a3? ♘d4!) 10 ... 0-0-0 and now:

a) **11 ♘d5** ♗xd2+ 12 ♘xd2 ♕e6 13 ♘f4 ♕f6 14 ♗e2 g5 15 ♘d5 ♕e6 16 0-0-0 ♔b8 17 ♗f3 ♘e5 (threatening ... ♘d3+) with a complicated game, Ackermann-Meyer, corres 1958. If 18 ♗e2 ♖d7 19 c5 Black regains the pawn with 19 ... ♘e4 20 ♘xe4 ♗xe4.

b) **11 ♗e2** ♗xc3 12 ♗xc3 ♘e4 13 0-0 ♖hg8 and 14 ... g5 has never occurred in practice. Black need hardly fear this variation.

8 ... ♗xc3
9 ♗xc3 ♗xe4
10 ♕d2 0-0
11 0-0-0

Now the natural 11 ... ♘c6? is bad: 12 c5! ♘f5 13 f3 ♕xd2+ 14 ♖xd2 ♘e3 15 fe ♘xf1 16 ♖e2 1-0, de Carbonnel-Starke, Leipzig 1953.

After the correct . . .

	11	...	♘d7 *(108)*

108
W

. . . the position is roughly equal. It is not possible to sketch out a universal plan for further play. An artificial demonstration game which shows a plausible course of events if White attacks on the king-side directly:

12	f3	♗g6
13	h4	h6
14	♘e2	♘c5
15	♘f4	♗h7
16	♘h5	♘e6
17	c5	♘f5
18	♕f2	♕e8
19	g4	♘e7
20	g5	♕a4
21	b3	

21 gh? ♕xa2 followed by . . .

♕b1+.

21	...	♕a3+
22	♕b2	♕xb2+
23	♔xb2	♗g6
24	♘g3	h5
25	b4	♘f5
26	♘xf5	♗xf5
27	♗d3	♗xd3
28	♖xd3	♖fd8
29	♖hd1	♔f8
30	♔c2	♔e7

½-½

This is only a single example as illustration; in a practical game there are naturally many other possibilities for both sides.

Summary

In the variation 4 ♕c2 Black has the choice between the particularly sharp continuation 4 ... d5 and the solid variation 4 ... ♗b4+. In all variations Black plays ... d5 and ... ♗f5 – the standard moves of this line. For White the set-ups with ed and ♘c3 are best. With that, general tips are almost exhausted. This variation is a tactical one; knowledge of concrete move orders is necessary.

8 Fajarowicz 4 ♘f3 and others

1	d4	♘f6
2	c4	e5
3	de	♘e4

In Chapter 6 we dealt with various queen moves on the d-file, in Chapter 7 the important variation 4 ♕c2. In this chapter we examine the main variation 4 ♘f3 and two other, rarely played, moves:

A 4 ♘d2 / 4 a3
B 4 ♘f3 ♘c6
C 4 ♘f3 ♗b4+

A1 4 ♘d2 ♘c5
A2 4 a3

A1

4 ♘d2 ♘c5 (109)

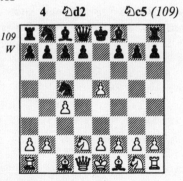

After 5 ♘gf3 ♘c6 the game transposes to B.

ECO gives 5 b4 ♘e6 6 a3 a5! 7 b5 d6 8 ed ♗xd6 9 ♘gf3 0-0 10 e3 ♘d7 with a good game for Black (the square c5 for the knight on e6, while the other comes to f6 or e5). 7 ... b6!? comes into consideration (instead of 7 ... d6) with the plausible follow-up 8 ♘gf3 ♗b7 9 e3 g5!? 10 ♗b2 ♗g7 11 ♕c2 (protecting the bishop on b2 in order to be able to capture the d-pawn after an eventual ... d6) 11 ... g4 12 ♘d4 ♘c5! (but not 12 ... ♗xe5?? 13 ♘xe6) 13 ♘e2 (the idea is protect the pawn on e5 and prepare ♘g3-f5) 13 ... d6 14 ♘g3 (14 ed ♗xb2 15 ♕xb2?? ♘d3+) 14 ... ♗xe5 15 ♗xe5 de and Black's position is preferable (the plan is ... ♕f6, ... ♘bd7, ... 0-0-0).

Certainly not everything has been played out in this variation, but on general strategic grounds Black must have a good game. The extra white pawn is weak and doubled and Black has a permanent strong point for his knight on c5.

A2

4 a3

This prevents the often unpleasant bishop check, but Black has a simple way of equalising.

Game 33
O'Kelly-Bisguier
San Juan 1969

(1 d4 ♘f6 2 c4 e5 3 de ♘e4)

4 a3 ♕h4
5 g3

On 5 ♗e3 Staker gives the following variation: 5 ... ♗c5 6 ♗xc5 ♘xc5 7 ♕c2 (7 e3 ♘c6 8 ♘f3 ♕e7 with equality; 9 ♕d5?! b6 followed by ... ♗b7 and moving the knight from c6 is favourable for Black) 7 ... ♘c6 8 ♘f3 ♕h5 9 e3 ♘xe5 10 ♗e2 d6 11 ♘bd2 ♗g4 with equality.

5 ... ♕h5
6 ♘d2

6 ♘f3 ♘c6 7 ♕c2 (7 ♗f4 ♗c5! 8 e3 g5) 7 ... ♕f5! (threatening ... ♘xg3). 7 ♘bd2 leads to the text.

6 ... ♘xd2
7 ♕xd2 ♘c6
8 ♘f3

8 f4?! is risky: 8 ... d6! 9 ed ♗xd6 10 e4 ♗g4 11 e5 ♗c5 followed by ... ♖d8 with a powerful initiative.

8 ... ♘xe5
9 ♕e3 d6
10 ♗g2 ♗e7
11 ♘xe5 ♕xe5
12 ♕xe5 de
½-½

Those who find this too quiet can try 7 ... ♕xe5 instead of 7 ... ♘c6, e.g. 8 ♘f3 ♕f6 9 ♗g2 g6 10 0-0 ♗g7. Here too the balance is maintained and there are still many pieces on the board. The game is quite open.

B

4 ♘f3 ♘c6 *(110)*

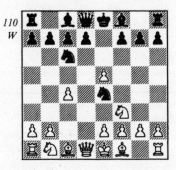

The two most common moves are:
B1 5 ♘bd2
B2 5 a3!
Others:

a) **5 ♗f4?** ♗c5 6 e3 ♗b4+ 7 ♘bd2 g5 8 ♗g3 h5 9 h3 ♘xg3 10 fg ♕e7 with advantage to Black.

b) **5 e3** d6 6 ed ♗xd6 7 ♘bd2 ♘c5 8 a3 ♕f6 9 ♘b3 ♘xb3 10 ♕xb3 ♗g4!, Strasdas-Richter, Berlin 1933. After 11 ♗e2 0-0-0 12 h3 ♗h5 followed by ... ♘e5 the situation was unclear but Black is certainly very active.

Snatching the pawn with 11 ♕xb7 does not turn out well: 11 ...

0-0 12 ♗e2 (12 ♕xc6?? ♗b4+) 12
... ♖ab8 13 ♕a6 ♘d4 (threatening
... ♗b4+ winning the queen) and
Black stands superbly, e.g. 14 ♕a4
♘xe2 15 ♔xe2 ♖xb2+! 16 ♗xb2
♕xb2+ 17 ♔d3 ♖d8 18 ♘d4 ♗c5
threatening both ... ♗f5+ and ...
♖xd4+.

c) 5 ♕d5 ♗b4+ 6 ♗d2 ♘xd2 7
♘bxd2 ♕e7 8 0-0-0 ♗xd2+ 9
♖xd2 and we have transposed
into Blümich-Fajarowicz, Chapter
6, C1. After 9 ... ♘b4 Black has
equalised.

B1

5   ♘bd2

Here it should be noticed that
this variation can also arise after
4 ♘d2 ♘c5 5 ♘gf3. Therefore you
should look at this section even if
you decide to play the variation
4 ... ♗b4+ (see C) instead of 4 ...
♘c6.

5   ...   ♘c5 *(111)*

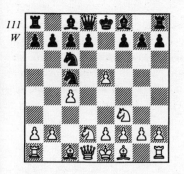

Here, too, the path divides, illus-
trated by practical examples.

B11 6 g3
B12 6 a3

B11

	6	g3	d6
	7	ed	♗xd6
	8	♗g2	0-0

9 0-0 ♕f6 10 ♘b3 ♗e6 11 ♘xc5
♗xc5 12 ♕a4 ♗g4 13 ♘g5 ♖ae8
14 ♘e4 ♖xe4 15 ♗xe4 ♗xe2 and
Black regains the exchange with a
good game, Barcza-Halić, Hungary
1946.

B12

	6	a3	♕e7

and now:

a) 7 b4? ♘xe5 8 e3 (8 ♘xe5 ♕xe5
with the double threat of ... ♘d3
mate and ... ♕xa1) 8 ... ♘cd3+
and Black stands better.

b) 7 e3 ♘xe5 8 ♘xe5 ♕xe5 9 ♘f3
♕f6 10 ♗e2 ♗e7 11 0-0 0-0 12
♘d4 ♘e6 13 ♘b5, Rejfir-Richter,
Prague 1931, and now 13 ... d6 14
♗f3 ♖d8 with equality. The following variation, naturally not forced,
demonstrates that this position
can quickly 'tip over': 15 ♖b1
(better is 15 ♘c3 immediately) 15
... c6 16 ♘c3 ♘g5 17 ♗e2 ♗f5 18
♗d3 ♘h3+! 19 gh (19 ♔h1? ♗xd3
20 ♕xd3 ♘xf2+) 19 ... ♕g6+ 20
♔h1 ♗xd3 21 ♖g1 ♗xb1 22 ♖xg6
♗xg6 and Black stands better.

B2

5   a3!

Prevents the usual freeing and pinning manoeuvre ... ♗b4+ and also a later ... ♘b4. Black now has problems.

5   ...   d6

What else? 5 ... a5 6 b3 d6 7 ♗b2 ♗e7 8 ♘bd2 ♘xd2 9 ♕xd2 with a healthy extra pawn for White.

6   ♕c2 (112)

112
B

After 6 ... d5 there follows 7 cd ♕xd5 8 ♘c3 ♘xc3 9 ♕xc3 ♗g4 10 ♗f4 and Black has scarcely anything for the pawn.

With regard to 6 ... ♗f5, see the following illustrative game:

Game 34
Reshevsky-Bisguier
New York 1954-5

(1 d4 ♘f6 2 c4 e5 3 de ♘e4 4 ♘f3 ♘c6 5 a3 d6)

	6	♕c2	♗f5
	7	♘c3	♘xf2
	8	♕xf5	♘xh1
	9	e6	fe
	10	♕xe6+	♕e7

11   ♕d5

The first storm is over and what are Black's prospects? Pretty bad. He cannot castle because of ♗g5. So:

	11	...	h6
	12	g3	g5

Again castling was not good on account of 13 ♘h4 ♕f6 (or 13 ... ♘xg3 14 hg ♕f6 15 ♘e4) 14 ♕xh1 followed by ♘d5. Therefore Black prevents ♘h4.

	13	♗g2	♘xg3
	14	hg (113)	

113
B

Castling is still denied to Black: 14 ... 0-0-0 15 ♘d4 with devastation on the h1-a8 diagonal. Black can still parry this threat but we see that in this game he can never act, but only react.

	14	...	♗g7
	15	♗h3	♘e5
	16	♗d2!	

16 ♕xb7 0-0 and Black still lives for a time.

	16	...	g4

17	♗xg4	h5
18	♗f5	c6
19	♕e4	♔d8
20	♘g5	♗f6
21	♘e6+	♔c8
22	0-0-0	♔b8
23	♗f4	b6
24	♔b1	1-0

After, for example, 24 ... ♔b7, 25 ♘b5 wins.

Summary

After 4 ♘f3, 4 ... ♘c6 is not good because of 5 a3. After 5 a3, the move 6 ♕c2 gains significantly in strength in comparison with lines in Chapter 6 (4 ♕c2), as neither ... ♗b4+ nor ... ♘b4 are possible.

C

	4	♘f3	♗b4+

We now examine:

C1 5 ♗d2
C2 5 ♘bd2

C1

	5	♗d2

Game 35
Smyslov-Steiner
Groningen 1946

(1 d4 ♘f6 2 c4 e5 3 de ♘e4 4 ♘f3 ♗b4+)

5	♗d2	♘xd2
6	♘bxd2	♘c6
7	a3	♗xd2+
8	♕xd2	♕e7
9	♕c3	*(114)*

114
B

	9	...	0-0?

The plan with kingside castling does not prove very good. A very important alternative comes into consideration here: 9 ... b6!? 10 e3 ♗b7 11 ♗e2 0-0-0 12 ♖d1 (12 0-0 ♖he8 and ... ♘xe5) 12 ... ♖de8! 13 ♖d5 g5!. Here Black can become active on the kingside with ... ♖hg8 or eventually regain the pawn on e5 by ♖g6-e6. There is still no practical experience of this plan.

10	♖d1	♖e8
11	♖d5	

Everything turns on regaining or holding the extra white pawn on e5. Now Black cannot attack this pawn again so he prepares to drive away the rook on d5.

11	...	b6
12	e3	♗b7
13	♗e2	♖ad8
14	0-0	♘b8

If the rook on d5 now moves Black achieves his aim: 15 ♖d2 ♗xf3 16 ♗xf3 ♕xe5 with equality according to Smyslov. The black knight is easily mobilised: ... d6 followed by ... ♘d7 etc.

After a notable exchange sacrifice . . .

| 15 | ♖c1! | ♗xd5 |
| 16 | cd | |

. . . White obtains an overwhelming advantage which he converts to a win by precise play:

16	...	d6
17	♗b5	♖f8
18	e4	a6
19	♗d3	de
20	♘xe5	♖d6 *(115)*

21	♘c4	♖h6
22	♘e3	♕h4
23	♕xc7	♖f6
24	g3	♕h5
25	e5	♖h6
26	h4	♕f3
27	♖c4	b5
28	♖f4	♕h5
29	♘g4	♖g6
30	♗xg6	♕xg6
31	e6	♕b1+
32	♔h2	f5

| 33 | e7 | ♖e8 |
| 34 | ♕d8 | |

1-0

So it didn't turn out well for Black. However Black could have chosen the plan with castling long on the 9th move. He is well advised to do this.

C2

| 5 | ♘bd2 *(116)* |

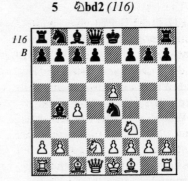

In my opinion the best variation for White.

| 5 | ... | ♘c6 |

Other moves are less good:

a) 5 ... f5 (suggested by Staker) 6 ef ♕xf6 7 ♘c2 and after the exchange on d2 White continues his development without problems and has a healthy extra pawn.

b) 5 ... d5 (*ECO*) 6 ed ♕xd6 and now 7 a3! ♗xd2+ 8 ♘xd2 (8 ♗xd2 ♕b6 9 e3 ♕xb2) and Black has almost nothing for the pawn.

| 6 | a3 | ♘xd2 |
| 7 | ♘xd2 | |

7 ab?! ♘xc4 is good for Black,

e.g. 8 b5 ♘6xe5; 8 ♕d5 ♘b6 9 ♕e4 ♕e7 10 ♗d2 d5! with advantage to Black.

The important alternative 7 ♗xd2 can lead to game 35 after 7 ... ♗xd2+ 8 ♕xd2 ♕e7 9 ♕c3. You should also remember here the plan with castling long: 9 ... b6 followed by ... ♗b7 and ... 0-0-0.

7 ... ♗f8

The lesser evil. 7 ... ♗xd2+ 8 ♗xd2 ♘xe5 9 ♗c3 gives White a lasting advantage in a position that is easy to play, e.g. 9 ... f6 10 e3 d6 11 ♗e2 0-0 12 0-0 ♗e6 13 b3 and White can slowly tighten his grip (plan: ♕c2, ♖ae1, e4, f4).

White's chances may still be somewhat better after the text continuation but in a complicated position a single inaccurate move is enough to lose the advantage.

As there are no examples from play of this attempted improvement we must be content with some constructed variations:

8	♘f3	♕e7
9	♗g5	♕e6
10	♕d5	h6
11	♗f4	g5
12	♗g3	♗g7
13	e3	

Naturally an exchange of queens either here or earlier will simply transpose.

13	...	b6
14	♗e2	♗b7
15	0-0	0-0-0 *(117)*

117 W

The game is unclear. Black now threatens 16 ... ♘xe5 17 ♕xe6 ♘xf3+. If here (or earlier) 16 ♘d4 then ... ♕xd5 followed by ... ♘xe5.

After 16 ♕xe6 de the following variations are plausible:

a) **17 ♖fd1** g4 18 ♘d4 ♘xe5 19 ♗xe5 ♗xe5 20 ♗xg4 c5 21 ♘b5

a1) **21 ... ♖dg8** 22 ♗h3 ♗f3 23 ♖d2 ♖xg2+ 24 ♗xg2 ♖g8 (with the winning threat 25 ... ♖xg2+ followed by ... ♖xh2) 25 ♘xa7+ ♔b8 26 ♖d8+! ♖xd8 27 ♗xf3 ♔xa7 28 ♖b1 ♖d2 and opposite bishops guarantee a draw.

a2) **21 ... ♗xb2** with unclear play.

b) **17 h3** ♘e7 18 ♘d4 ♘g6 19 f4 gf 20 ♗xf4 ♗xe5 with roughly equal play. Less good would be 20 ... ♘xe5 21 ♗xe5 ♗xe5 22 ♖xf7 ♗xd4 23 ed ♖xd4 24 ♗g4!.

Summary

In the Fajarowicz Gambit sharp variations arise after queen sorties on the 4th move which are certainly playable for Black. Here tactics rule over strategy; there are no general plans: whoever is familiar with the most important variations of the material at hand will have excellent chances in a game.

4 ♘f3 is the most unpleasant for Black. A complicated, strategic struggle arises, though still with tactical elements. Black has practical chances in positions where the pawn on e5 is put under slow siege, as is discussed in detail in the foregoing chapter.

9 Declining the Gambit

1	d4	♘f6
2	c4	e5

Declining the gambit very rarely occurs in practice. Here is a collection of the known examples:

A 3 e3
B 3 ♗g5
C 3 e4
D 3 d5
E 3 ♘f3

A

3	e3	ed
4	ed	♗b4+
5	♗d2	♗xd2+
6	♘xd2	0-0
7	♗d3	d5
8	♘e2	♗g4
9	0-0	♘c6
10	f3	♗h5 $\overline{\overline{+}}$

Vistaneckis-Vajda, Prague 1931. Black plays ... ♖e8 and ... ♗g6 and exerts pressure on White's central pawns, e.g. ... dc followed by ... ♘d5 and doubling on the d-file.

B

3	♗g5	ed
4	♕xd4	♗e7
5	♘f3	♘c6
6	♕d1	♘e4
7	♗xe7	♕xe7
8	a3	d6
9	e3	0-0
10	♗e2	♕f6
11	♘bd2	♗f5 $\overline{\overline{+}}$

Ladmann-Tartakower, Scarborough 1929. After 12 ♘xe4 ♗xe4 13 ♕d2 ♖ad8 14 0-0 d5 Black is obviously more active.

C

3	e4	♘xe4 (118)

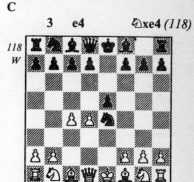

118
W

4   de

4 ♕e2 ♗b4+ 5 ♘d2 ♘xd2 6 ♕xe5+ ♗e7! 7 ♗xd2 0-0 followed by ... ♗f6 and ... ♖e8 $\mp$.

4   ...   ♗c5

Now Schlechter gives:

a) **5 ♘h3 d6 6 ♕e2 f5 7 ef 0-0!** 8 fg ♖e8 9 ♗e3 ♗xe3 10 fe ♗xh3 11 gh ♕h4+ and wins.

b) **5 ♘h3 d6 6 ♕d5 f5 7 ef ♘xf6** followed by ... 0-0 and later ... ♗xh3 or, if ♘h3-f4, ... ♘g4.

c) **5 ♕d5 ♗xf2+ 6 ♔e2 f5 7 ef ♘xf6 8 ♕e5+ ♔f7** with advantage to Black (9 ♔xf2?? ♘g4+; 9 ♔d1 ♖e8).

D

3   d5   ♗c5
4   ♘c3   d6 *(119)*

Now:

a) **5 ♕c2 c6 6 ♘f3 0-0 7 ♗g5** (7 e4? ♘g4) **7 ... ♘bd7 8 e3 ♕c7 9 ♗d3 h6 10 ♗h4 ♗b4 11 dc bc 12 0-0 ♗b7** is good for Black (plan: ... d5; 13 e4 ♘h5 and ... ♘f4).

b) **5 e4 c6 6 ♗d3** (6 ♘f3 ♗g4) **6 ... cd 7 cd a6 8 ♘f3 ♘bd7 9 0-0** (9 ♗g5 h6 10 ♗h4 ♘f8 followed by ... ♘g6 and eventually ... ♘h5-f4 square for the knight!) **9 ... 0-0 10 ♗g5 h6 11 ♗h4 b5** and in IM Minev's opinion Black is better (plan: ... ♕b6, ... ♗b7, ... ♖c8 with play on the queenside).

E

3   ♘f3   ed
4   ♘xd4   d5
5   cd

On 5 ♘c3? Black has 5 ... c5 followed by ... d4.

5   ...   ♕xd5
6   ♘c3   ♗b4
7   ♕a4+   ♘c6
8   ♘xc6   ♗xc3+
9   bc   ♗d7!
10   ♘b4   ♗xa4
11   ♘xd5   ♘xd5

According to Carl Schlechter, Black has more than enough compensation for the opponent's bishop pair in his better pawn structure and open lines after ... 0-0-0.

Index of Variations

Fajarowicz Gambit

Index of Complete Games